Wave as you pass

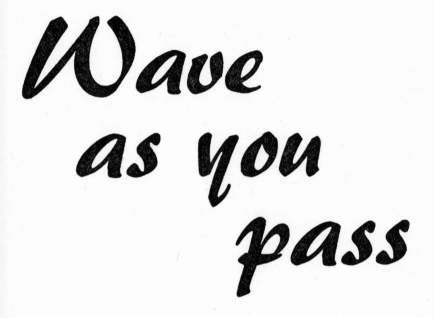

Wave as you pass

HARRY LEE NEAL

J. B. LIPPINCOTT COMPANY
Philadelphia and New York

for
Allison

CONTENTS

Illustrations, from photographs, following page 86

THE MIDNIGHT RIDE

The phone exploded in my ear.

"What are you doing in Missouri?" cried our personal manager from Atlanta. "Your Canadian tour starts tomorrow night!"

As Nelson and Neal, Australian-American two-piano team, my wife and I had struggled into Springfield, Missouri, with the expectation of several days' hard-earned rest. But now we were stunned by the discovery that curtain time in Fort William, Ontario, was 25 hours and 955 miles away!

This was March, 1954, when concert schedules had carried us back and forth through the black heart of a Midwestern dust storm. A Sunday-night call from Springfield to Ralph Bridges, our manager in Atlanta, had brought incredible news: Springfield had been placed on our original schedule through an error, since corrected in fairly ample time. The dreadful complication was that a new, corrected itinerary, sent us by air mail, had never been delivered because planes were unable to land in the dust storm.

Now, without final calculations, I knew that the truck which carried us, our infant son and two concert grand pianos, would need to roll all night and all the next day in order to reach Fort William before concert time. Then, regardless of our need for sleep, we would have to unload pianos and appear on stage immediately, giving no impression but that of strength, poise, skill and artistic temperament. We could not simply catch a plane to Fort William, because we had to furnish our pianos for that concert as well as those on the following nights.

At best, concertizing is a hard life physically. We are told that the act of performing requires as much energy as digging a ditch, building a stone fence, or chopping logs. There are some hundred thousand notes involved in a two-piano concert, each of which requires from two ounces to thirty pounds of pressure for perform-

3

ance. Every bit of this enormous physical exertion must be co-ordinated with a technical control which the layman might find difficult to conceive. Small wonder that pianists work up a sweat!

Aside from the actual playing, Allison and I normally drive from one to three hundred miles per day, load and unload our two specially matched concert grand pianos, care for our three children, who travel with us, and practice—plus making all the business and social contacts necessary in each city where we play. But we have learned to enjoy this schedule. What we have *not* learned to enjoy are the incidental hazards: pianos are dropped, tires blow out, wheels break down and motors blow up in places like Fishtrap, Kentucky.

Still, we had never canceled an engagement except once, when our truck turned over on a sheet of ice. And although ice was the most dangerous hazard for our truck, the dust storms just behind us had been the most trying personal experience we had yet known.

For two weeks we agonized through this storm. Much of the time I could see nothing through the windshield; Allison stared straight down from a side window, calling out our position in re-lation to the edge of the pavement—my only driving guide. The eerie gloom was so dense that street lights were turned on in midday at Dumas, Texas. South of Scott City, Kansas, we had been terrified as 85-mile-an-hour gusts slid us back and forth over a deserted highway lubricated and slimy with snow and dust.

When we finally reached Springfield, Missouri, our spare tire and wheel had both been ruined but not replaced; I had let my money get dangerously low. We expected and needed the half week's rest promised by our schedule. Now suddenly a phone call shattered our complacence. Catastrophe stared us in the face: an important audi-ence nearly a thousand miles away was expecting us to appear before them only hours later.

I heard Ralph resign himself to the impossibility of the situation: "Which one of us will call them to say you can't make it?"

Somehow this acceptance of defeat electrified me—an irresistible challenge. Driving 40,000 miles to nearly a hundred cities each winter, Allison and I had developed a firm show-must-go-on phi-losophy. Although there had never been anything comparable to this situation, we liked to imagine ourselves equal to any emer-gency. Moreover, we now learned that the Fort William date had been set fifteen months earlier. Failure to present ourselves there would be a serious indication of irresponsibility.

I hardly paused before replying, "Neither. We'll get there." And if we didn't, it would be a glorious try.

By 7:00 p.m. the telephone poles lining Highway 65 were flickering past our headlights. Munching on a sandwich while driving, I immediately began mental calculations. We had 955 miles to go and would lose an hour crossing the time zone. The trip must be made in twenty-two hours to give us two and a half hours to unload pianos, tune them, grab a bite, rest (!) and dress. An ambitious schedule.

Nine hundred and fifty miles in twenty-two hours. That came to an average of just over forty-three miles an hour. I knew from experience that we required a ten-minute gas stop every two hours, which left us only fifty-five minutes' driving time per hour. This meant we must actually average forty-*seven* miles an hour. Adding a minimum allowance for odd delays dictated that we keep the speedometer at over fifty for twenty-two hours.

This may not sound too imposing for an average automobile driver. But the gravity of that situation for us is borne home by the fact that our absolute top, boiler-busting speed was around fifty-*five* miles an hour. We had to go slam-bang wide open for twenty-two hours!

The enormity of what we had taken on staggered me. We faced a long and concentrated endeavor. I had only $20 in my pocket. We had no spare tire and no spare wheel to put one on. For twenty-two hours a Damoclean sword was to hang over our heads: one flat tire would completely finish our little experiment in impossibilities. Of course this omits mentioning the more obvious difficulties. After driving for twenty-two hours, if we made it, there was a concert to play. Professional truckers would consider this marathon drive to be quite a feat. After it, could the truck driver turn concert pianist? Unlikely, but he had to.

Automatically, I returned the greeting of a motorist who honked cheerily in response to a whimsical sign painted on the back of my truck: "You're behind Nelson and Neal—Wave As You Pass!" Watching him pull by, I vowed resolutely that precious few people would pass us *this* night!

By the stroke of midnight we had reached Chillicothe, Missouri, right on schedule. Traces of snow and our old friend, the dust storm, spoke to us occasionally, but otherwise driving was clear. Every six minutes found us five miles nearer to Canada. My eyes described an endless and often exciting circle: road, speedometer, watch, road, speedometer, watch. The motor roared, and we hurtled through the night toward a goal now only seventeen hours away. Our baby slept as a baby should, and my poor Allison slept as best she could.

At 2:15 a.m. some 65,000 persons lay asleep in Fort William-Port Arthur, Ontario, with no inkling of the struggle we were making to reach them. Perhaps a few turned over to snuggle deeper in their blankets as we left Lucas, Iowa, close behind a large truck.

For the next hour this truck kept us behind schedule on the one hand, while trampling my spirits on the other. I memorized the sign on its rear, knew its license number by heart, and had even chuckled grimly over the *"If you can read this, you're too darn close!"* sign. At the edge of Des Moines he halted before me for a stop sign and right turn. Seeing a long-closed filling station on the corner to our right, I rashly pulled across this lot, cutting off the corner and the truck as well. Now at last I could make up the lost time and get back on our precious schedule!

Moments later, a siren's wail summoned me to the curb. Two exceedingly courteous officers asked to see my driver's license and explained that they had observed my maneuver; while by no means illegal, it was nonetheless a breach of good manners, and they hoped I would not allow haste to obscure good judgment because that was how people got hurt, and they wished me to enjoy my stay in Des Moines and Iowa, however brief. And on and on.

Those gentlemen did a fine public relations job for the city of Des Moines. But alas, while they spoke my trucker friend zoomed past. My heart sank as I realized he must be contended with all over again, though perhaps more conservatively next time.

At 6:15 a.m. Allison took over on the Minnesota line. When I awoke to drive three hours later, we were in the outskirts of St. Paul, and a lovely snow was falling. The soft white flakes aroused memories of a childhood conviction that men were very, very old indeed when they no longer believed snow to be the most beautiful sight in all of creation. I seemed distinctly jaded.

Although our drive to Duluth was painful, we counted out thirty-one more five-mile units of six minutes each. Snow rendered the highway treacherous, our stomachs yammered for food, and my eyes were soaked in fatigue.

Highway 61 from Duluth toward the Canadian line proved a revelation. Lake Superior's northern shore boasts spectacular scenery in abundance, but it has precious few Standard Oil stations open in the month of March. Having bought sandwiches and some gas on the way up, our $20 had by now been reduced to $6.50. It was imperative that we purchase gasoline on our credit card, but there were almost no stations at all, let alone the kind we needed.

In one settlement I bought a dollar's worth of gas to eke our way to a Standard station "about ten miles up the road." It was nearer thirty, but we made it. From there I placed a call to our contact in Fort William, telling him simply that we had been held up and would not arrive until six in the evening. He was charmingly co-operative.

"Where did you come from?"

"Oh, we left Minneapolis about 9:00 this morning." True, we had; why bother him with our troubles?

Finally, at 5:15 p.m. we reached the Canadian border, exhausted, but only forty-two miles from our destination. "This time," I said with a great sigh, "we really *have* been through all mortal man can stand: there can be no further test."

But there was.

It happens that there is no duty chargeable to musical instruments carried by concert artists over the border of our good Neighbor on the North. This fine point of law is successfully hidden in section such-and-such of book so-and-so. The Canadian officials, though cordial, appeared never to have heard of it. When they discovered our two Baldwin concert grands (valued at $15,000), we were refused permission to cross the border until several thousand dollars' bond had been produced. For forty-five frantic minutes I stood in that little room on first one foot and then the other, watching the clock tick away minutes we had fought so desperately to earn. At last, bond was secured on credit and we hastened toward our truck and Fort William.

"Now, surely," moaned Allison, "we have stood 'the most.'"

Delivering her at the Fort William hotel at 7:20, I rushed off, promising to return.

But it was decreed otherwise. Our auditorium was on a second floor, and delicate, 1,300-pound pianos are not to be rushed up stairs. Maintaining a hard-come-by smile (I tried to, anyway) I spent until 8:15 getting those pianos on stage. Most of the audience had arrived by that time, and would probably have been shocked to realize that the artist they had come to hear was none other than the most disreputable-looking member of the loading crew!

Back at the hotel, Allison ordered an enormous meal for each of us. Sadly she watched mine grow cold, packed up a few biscuits for me, and went to the concert hall. There she quickly checked the pianos' tuning while I changed clothes and shaved. My hands were shaking with hunger and fatigue; I tried to relax and get a grip on myself.

Before leaving the dressing room we paused to swear that having been through such an unholy ordeal in order to present ourselves here, we must now give a concert worthy of the name. It was unthinkable that we should have struggled so insanely for a merely mediocre performance. On this night, regardless of all that had gone before, Allison and I must give a performance of which we might always be proud.

Right on time at 8:30, we marched to our position behind the curtain, trying to look sublimely unconcerned with it all.

But Fate had one last jest up her sleeve. As we stood there, Ken Potter casually reminded us, "Of course you'll play 'God Save the Queen.'" God save my soul! Such a thought had never crossed our minds! This was our first Canadian concert, and we had not known to prepare the anthem in two-piano form. Allison (who is Australian and had had supper besides) quickly saved the day. She marched out, bold as brass, played "God Save the Queen," and came back calmly observing that she would "rehearse it properly tomorrow."

After two deep breaths we strode out to begin the Bach. Music is a worthy religion, and that night it answered our prayers.

When the last bow had been taken, Mr. Potter made another casual (though far more endearing) remark. "Would you two like to come out for a couple of steaks?" We would; we did; and (only because food has that effect on me) I began to feel drowsy.

Before going to bed, Allison and I chattered excitedly. Time and again we had been forced into the wringer of life's washing

A TWIG IS BENT

machine, each time believing "This is the most we can possibly take; anything more would be impossible!" But each time the realization had come that "impossible" simply means "I quit" and is defeated only by not quitting.

I remember standing there in my bvd's, exclaiming over and over, "We won't say it. This is *not* the most we can do. I feel as though I could get in that truck right now and do it all over again!" Of course we could, echoed Allison. (Then we went to bed.)

These words are the first Fort William will know of our adventures in reaching them. One of the most gratifying reviews of our entire career appeared in the Fort William *Daily Times-Journal* on March 23, 1954. It described us as having played "an empirical and secure program," with "a fastidious nonchalance that is in reality concentrated endeavor." Our performance, they said, had "made musical history."

If they only knew.

I am the first professional musician to occur in the Neal family.

According to my father, our forebears maintained an unbroken record of indifference to all forms of musical expression, and hearing today's Neal clan sing on Sunday morning arouses no doubts as to his veracity. On her side, Mother can recall only one distant uncle who played fiddle at neighborhood barn dances; we assume it is from this direction that my musical instincts come.

On both sides, my ancestors were farming people, all more or less native to Henry County in northwestern Tennessee.

Granddad Neal claimed that we are descendants of the Scottish clan MacNeill. He also insisted on an altogether unnecessary footnote that a common Virginia hanging launched our branch of the family. A hanging for murder might have carried with it a certain element of prestige and dignity, but the ignominy of a MacNeill being strung up for horse stealing was more than his immediate family could stand. They packed up their belongings and headed over the mountains for Tennessee, changing their name to Neal on the way.

Great-granddad William Franklin Neal was a little one-eyed man who lived on a farm about eleven miles from Paris in Henry County, Tennessee. I can barely remember childhood expeditions to the ruins of our ancient homeplace, located on an idyllic knoll in beautifully rolling woodland. I was always half afraid to go inside the old cabin, for decaying logs and crumbling fireplace brought up the ghosts of forgotten laughter and of sweaty men who had toiled there long before. Outside in the sunlight, long-neglected flower beds still had scrawny blossoms poking up through an overgrowth of brambles and weeds.

Great-granddad did not believe in the Civil War, and he had the courage of his convictions. He retired to this cabin during the War,

13

brandishing his muzzle-loader, and daring the recruiting gangs of either army to come and get him. Here my grandfather was born, and among these ancient oaks the young boy learned to "bark" squirrels: shooting at the limb underneath in order to kill his quarry by concussion, rather than damaging its body with a direct shot.

Tennessee was frontier country in the early nineteenth century, and abounded in a wild post-Revolutionary admiration for all things French. When this land west of the Tennessee River was opened up to settlers in 1818, it was only natural that the Henry County seat (in which I have always resided) should be called Paris. Lafayette was the most popular middle name a boy could possess at that time; as late as 1900 every schoolroom here had at least one 'Fayette, local custom finally shortening the name to "Fate." Grand-dad was one of these: William Lafayette Neal, called "Fate." He was the last of his breed, too, for World War I came along and many local boys went to see France at first hand. When they came back home no more children were called Lafayette.

I remember Granddad only as warts about the eyes and a shiny bald head which presided over occasional Sunday dinners. His early desire had been to study law, but before going to college he took a temporary farm job for a year. As many another boy has discovered, such temporary jobs become permanent; he ended life a farmer and a Baptist lay minister.

My Dad, William Fisher Neal, fulfilled his father's ambition and became a lawyer. He was born with a passionate regard for facts, and this proved an excellent basis for his profession. It prompted his hobby of local history, and his insistence upon hard and un-varnished truth makes him an admirable testing ground for new ideas. Once an idea has passed through the gauntlet of his criticism with approval, it is ready for the world.

I have never seen my father open his mouth for the purpose of carrying a tune. Sometimes he does whistle, but these occasions represent little gain to society. The only tune he ever attempts is a drab, five-note phrase, which has remained unchanged since the days of my infancy. On the other hand, his humor has a softness which I find appealing. As a child I asked at the breakfast table, "Is it dark inside the sugar bowl, Dad?"

"Yes, son."

"Is it dark inside the closet?"

"Yes, son."

"Is it dark inside my head, Dad?"

With a smile, "Yes, son. It's *very* dark inside your head."

Contrasted with Dad's native love of facts and history, Mother was never one to find interest in the past, and devotes herself to more problematical and imaginative speculation. She can brush off her family history in short order: her name is Ellen, and the family's, Willingham; they were farmers. She and her mother wandered back and forth between Tennessee and Texas. In 1923 she married my father, and has been his secretary ever since.

To which we might add that they had three children. Bill came first, then Bobby (who later died), and on May 12, 1928, I finished the family.

I am now thirty years old, and in looking back I see my life divided into three fairly equal portions. The first of these, during which I had no formal musical education, lasted almost until my ninth birthday.

My earliest recollections are those in which we boys were urged to appreciate beauty, cultivate imagination and develop curiosity. Mother taught well, and we, like most children, were fertile ground for such ideas.

Our home was a white, two-story affair, about a mile from town, and Mother used it for my first lessons in esthetic balance. She pointed out how the large center structure was balanced by two identical wings, one on either side. A few feet beyond each end of the house grew a tall poplar, and trudging up the dirt road on a summer evening, I would gaze at the silhouette and wonder, Who else in all the world ever lived in such a beautiful place?

We did not have many material things, but Mother held flowers under our noses, pointed out trees and birds, sent us racing out of the house to watch sunsets, woke us up in the middle of the night to see an eclipse of the moon, and made us wonder at birds' nests and anthills. She would turn out the lights and open the door of our coal stove, so that a newly hung Christmas tree might sparkle in the flames' flickering light.

"These things are not beautiful in themselves," she would say.

"Rather, they are merely keys which unlock the beauty hiding inside each of you."

We had few toys, so Mother substituted imagination. An eroded gulley became Yellowstone National Park; cardboard boxes were the speediest of racing cars. At night there was a family institution of the "few." Bill and I would clamber into bed with Mother for a *few* minutes before bedtime, and we all imagined together what we would do "when our ship came in." There in the twilight were designed boats which would not roll when buffeted by waves, hammers which extracted nails without bending them, and submarines (for use in a neighbor's nearby pond).

"Mother, what happens when people grow old?"

"They lose their curiosity," came the most useful of answers. "All young people are curious, but old people usually stop asking questions, and just want things 'the way they always were.' Children—" she weighed her words—"never reject new things simply because they are new, and never stop asking questions. '*Why?*' is the most honorable word in the English language."

And she made it so. No question was ever ignored, or allowed to pass unanswered. If I interrupted an adult conversation, the question might be deferred until later, but a satisfactory answer was always forthcoming. The answers were never beyond my understanding and when I asked, "Why are little boys and girls different?" I was quite satisfied to learn that it was "so you can tell them apart"!

To Mother's love of beauty, imagination and curiosity, I brought Dad's quality of unyielding persistence, otherwise known as stubbornness. Persistence, wedded to imagination and curiosity, caused Mother to record one portion of a two-hour interrogation to which I subjected her one rainy afternoon when I was five.

"How much money will it take to build a secret cabin?"

"That depends on how much material you use, like boards and nails."

"Well, how many boards would it take?"

"Goodness, I don't know."

"Well, guess."

"Oh, I wouldn't know how to begin."

"Well, guess anyway."

"If your boards were a foot wide, and the cabin six feet square, there might be twenty-four boards in the walls."

"See how easy it was, Mother?"

Then followed a long quiz on bracing, flooring, and how much longer the roof boards would have to be because of roof pitch and eaves. Having disposed of boards, I turned to nails.

"How many nails would it take for the cabin, Mother?"

"Heavens, child, I've no idea."

"Well, how many times would you nail a board?"

"Lord. I suppose three nails would hold each end, with maybe one or two in the middle."

"Would I waste many nails, Mother? I mean, how many would I bend?"

For two hours this cross-examination went on, and today we still have the plans I drew up with Mother, specifying the exact length and number of boards, the exact number of nails, and the exact amount of roofing, etc., required for a secret cabin. Similar plans exist for a submarine and a sailboat, in case there is any current market for these items.

My stubbornness also caused me to abuse Mother's respect for the question, "Why?" It finally got to the point that I could never be told to do anything whatsoever without hedging and stalling with, "But why?"

At breakfast one morning, it was announced that Frank Buck was planning to take four Eagle Scouts on his next animal-hunting expedition in the Malayan jungles. Bill and I announced our intention to join the Boy Scouts and go with him.

"But, Harry," Dad turned to me, "Frank Buck wouldn't take you."

"Why?"

"Because you're undisciplined and won't do what you're told."

"Oh, but I'd do *anything* Frank Buck told me to!"

"No, he'd see a tiger about to jump on you, and would holler for you to fall down on the ground, and you would just turn around and say, 'But *why?*' "

I knew it was true. There were many wonderful things about my childhood, but discipline was not one of them.

Thirteen thousand miles away, an imperious voice cracked through the morning air.

"Children, stand still!"

Three little statues froze beside a dusty road, and the woman watching them felt her heart freeze also. In an agony of suspense she prayed that they would not try to run when they saw the deadly Brown Snake, then only inches from the shoes of her eldest child. Australia is a land as large as the United States, and has few non-poisonous snakes; about some there is a saying, "You're dead ten minutes before they bite you," for the Death Adder is almost invariably fatal. Not a sound stirred the air, nor could any motion be seen, save that of a six-foot reptile gliding past May Nelson's three small children. They came from strong stock: their father's people had always been Swedish sea-captains, and their mother's iron will demonstrated amply why her Cornish ancestors were the only people in England never defeated by William the Conqueror. Now the stillness was unnatural, but with no sudden motion to startle the deadly Brown Snake into activity, it soon passed under a fence and disappeared.

Discipline had paid off.

It never occurred to me that we were poor. Brother Bill and I played with two boys who lived next to us, named Charles and Buddy Raines, and sometimes we would all go over the hill to the little settlement behind our houses and play with the colored kids. I once saw those little dark children eating a pie made of mud smeared over watermelon rinds which we had thrown out, and that became my standard of being poor.

We wrestled and ran with them, and one day they accorded us the signal honor of taking us into a small shanty to view Willie, the victim of a "cuttin' fight." This young man's torso, cheeks, throat and arms were all swathed in heavy bandages. He seemed proud of our interest and gave a vivid description of his fight, dwelling particularly on the charms of a lady-love who was the cause of it all. I had been collecting Shirley Temple pictures for some time, and now began to feel apprehensive about where it was all going to lead. Finally, to cap off his remarks, he had the bandages pulled back from his "best" gashes; we stared with wide eyes and open mouths, agreeing that we'd never heard of *anybody* who'd *ever* had such a beautiful cutting.

By fall he had recovered from his wounds, and immediately undertook to leave a mark on my eating habits for all time. When hog-killing season came around, I heard the squealing and went to watch. It was all over when I got there, for they were stringing the carcass up to a limb. I have since questioned Willie's finesse as a butcher, but his sense of theatrics was masterful: My stomach flipped over as he plunged a huge knife into the pig's belly and ripped it open. Then, looking about for a suitable container, he held the guts in with one hand and yelled, "Mammy, run fetch me a tub to catch these chit'lings!"

I have not eaten chitterlings since that day, nor do I ever expect to in the future.

When we had money enough to hire help, Lee Dora would come over the hill and keep house for us. Many were the hurt feelings and barked shins which I cried away on her ample black bosom. Wood ticks got rather bad one summer, and she had to poke through our hair every evening to remove the fellow-travelers we had picked up during the day. I discovered this was an intensely pleasurable experience. She worked slowly, parting the hair tuft by tuft, and at every slight motion on my scalp a new wave of sensual goose bumps would sweep over me. Finally our tick menace died down, and the regular examinations were suspended. I was desolate. Soon I hit upon the simple expedient of pulling ticks from the ears of neighborhood dogs and installing them in my hair. It worked for a time, but soon Lee Dora noticed that all my new ticks were running around loose with chunks of dog flesh still in their jaws. The examinations were suspended again, this time permanently. Today I always have my hair washed professionally and though I switch from barber to barber, twenty-five years have gone by without anyone recapturing the magic of Lee Dora's slow fingers threading across my scalp.

Mozart, in spite of the prettified picture we have today, was a rowdy boy; he was full of tricks, wrote off-color jokes home to his parents and believed in a roaring good time. If only these were the sure attributes of musical greatness! My career would have been made from then on.

We were not quiet children. One of the most difficult transitions to living in town, where we moved when I was eight, was learning to speak quietly enough that people wouldn't hear us in the next house.

While we were still out in the country, we saw *Life Begins at 40,* a Will Rogers movie featuring hog-calling. Bill and I came home at eleven that night yelling, "Pig-a-hoooey!" out our bedroom window at the tops of our voices. Presently an answering cry of some sort came through the woods, and we had a fine time until hoarseness set in. Next morning four different neighbors called on Mother, after waiting until Dad had left for the office. They asked discreetly if he had been mistreating her, and if there was anything they could do. Our hog-calling adventures came to an abrupt conclusion.

Mother was a pretty fair psychologist.

In the evenings she read Bible and Uncle Remus stories to the neighborhood boys, always locking the front door before beginning, and always reading the Bible story first. That order of procedure was arrived at the hard way: if she did not lock the door first, the boys would not arrive until just in time for the Uncle Remus, and if she read the Uncle Remus first, they would suddenly discover their mothers wanted them to come home early, before the Bible story began.

When we asked for a rifle, she neither gave us one nor refused to give us one. Instead she impressed on us the dangerous nature of the weapon, and had us agree to earn the gun by spending one whole year without even pretending to shoot another child in play. It seemed quite fair, and the first thing we did was to run out and brag before the neighborhood boys about our arrangement. They were hungry with envy, and therein lay our downfall. Little boys are always pointing and going "Bang!" and there are always angry brothers or envious neighborhood kids to run and tell Mother about it. Mother kept a special calendar, and after each offense, she soberly marked off the days to the end of our *new* year; to this day I have never owned a rifle nor blamed anyone for it but myself.

Smoking, however, we took in our own hands. Charles, Buddy, Bill and I would wander up and down a nearby highway collecting "tobies" (cigarette butts) and would smoke them (appropriately) in the smokehouse, where all the hams and vegetables were stored; we always ate onions afterwards to kill the smell. Once Bill came to me and said, "Let's go see if we can find some cigarettes." We marched off into the woods, and I was amazed by the quickness with which he was able to find a small sack containing cigarettes and matches under a large tree. We forgot to eat onions this time, and Mother whaled the tar out of us when we got home.

Early next day she announced that we might smoke under her supervision, and sat us down with a large number of cigarettes. "Let's smoke them all," she suggested. Somehow it didn't seem so much fun any more, but we smoked one after another, with Mother constantly urging us on. Presently I began to feel wretched and looked at Bill, who was positively green; together we rose and ran for the woods. Neither of us has ever smoked since, though I have always retained an uncommon fondness for onions.

Mother told us that vitamins, and all the "good," were in the skin of vegetables. Today I never peel apples, and always enjoy the skin of baked potatoes.

Perhaps she cheated, ever so slightly, when it came to carrots. They, she said, would make us see in the dark. We were often sent —armed with a bunch of carrots—to the pitch-black coal closet beside our heating stove. Inside, we would munch and peer, munch and peer. Gradually, as our eyes became accustomed to the darkness, we began to see each other, and ate more and more furiously as new objects became visible. Often we called for new supplies of carrots and tore away at them, unaware of the silent laughter outside.

Today, we humans enjoy the pleasant fantasy that modern society is the first to enjoy the benefits of psychology. However, it is well to remember the Sioux Indians, who told their children that butterfly wings smeared over their hearts would enable them to run fleetly as antelopes. Any boy who sets out to catch a dozen butterflies, without benefit of a net, is going to be a middling good runner by the time summer is out.

In my sixth year, I entered the first grade without any recognizable interest in music. While in bed during a spell of illness, I had persuaded Mother to teach me nursery songs, and sometimes sang myself to sleep with them. All our family slept in the same room, however, and on this one point I was soon curbed. My injured feelings were due, I confess, not to my frustrated musical excursions, but to the bluntness of my being told to shut up. Sometimes I banged on a piano over at Charles and Buddy's house, but always became vexed at the crude sounds I produced, and never pursued it very far.

One day at school the class was shuffled into another room, and we were given a music lesson. Our teacher, Miss Kathryn Adams, was the first pretty woman I had ever seen, and I was thoroughly smitten by both her and music. She suggested that we sing and dance when out of school, and while on the way home with some hardheaded little country boys, I proposed that we do so. They co-operated for a short time and then announced that they were through; I insisted, and a brief scuffle ensued. To be blunt, they beat the daylights out of me, and, with Willie and his "cuttin' fight" in mind, I decided that neither Miss Adams nor music was worth it.

Shortly afterward, we went to see Sonja Henie's first movie, and I was so enamored that I made up a poem about her and set it to music. At the time, I was experimenting quite a bit with Mother's typewriter, and devised a simple method for typing my melodies on paper. I indicated notes with an "x," rolled the paper up and down to show changes of pitch, and used the space bar to suggest various time values. The result was a rough rule of thumb from which I could always recall the melody later on. A couple of years later I was to do just that, and put my "Dancing On Ice" song about Miss Henie to good use.

I attached only moderate importance to my song. So far as I was concerned, the great landmark in my first-grade experience was the first occasion on which I ever had to defend myself in public.

It was over a picture I had drawn. The class was regularly furnished pots of paint and large sheets of paper to which the paint was lustily applied. This was called an art class, and was supposed to develop something or other. After a time, I frankly set out to do a masterpiece. It took me several days, as I recall, and was a fair-sized picture of a boy lying on a hillside watching an airplane fly through the cloudy sky. In a valley below the hill could be seen a small carnival and an animal cage in which Clyde Beatty was subduing a lion. I could not leave well enough alone, and finally put a picket fence around the hill.

When the great day came, Miss Newberry stood me before the class to unveil my work, but instead of praise and admiration, I was met by a squalling storm of derision.

"He's drawn the sky all the way down to the ground!"

I don't know how it is today, but when I was in the first grade, the sky was always a blue streak across the top of the paper. Everything between it and the horizon was blank, for the useful purpose of suggesting that the sky was up in the air and that we were not.

I had been proud of my innovation, and had carefully colored the sky right down to the ground all across my picture.

Nearly overpowered with ridicule, I looked to Miss Newberry for help. Wisely, she risked my outrage by forcing me to fight my battles alone. It was a fairly grim one; children are not kind, and I didn't know what to do or say, except insist that I *felt* it that way. Suddenly (I was long enough in thinking of the obvious) I had an inspiration and pointed at the window.

"Look! See for yourself!" I cried. "The sky *does* come down to the ground!"

Bedlam broke loose. Over half the class swarmed out of their seats and rushed to the windows; a few came over to inspect my picture more closely; one hurried to the bathroom, and most of the rest stood up on top of their desks, for some reason which I have never yet divined. I had the wild satisfaction of hearing a chorus of agreeing voices, with only one or two bitter-enders grumbling, "I don't care. The sky is *still* up in the air!" Breathless, I glanced at Miss Newberry and caught her unawares. She was looking up in the air, chuckling to herself. It was years before I could understand why.

These were the golden days when I should have begun to study the piano.

On the other side of the world, another six-year-old was having artistic difficulties. Auditioning for a new teacher, little Allison Nelson demonstrated her sense of "perfect pitch." Then, in performance, she played a wrong note; it was obviously a serious matter, and she crawled under the dining-room table to cry away her shame. A box of candy soon patched things up, and Jessica Dix was delighted to have a new pupil straining for perfection this early in the game. The right teacher had found the right child at the right moment.

The first years of a young lawyer's career are usually referred to as his "starvation period." I am not sure whether this little truism found its origin in the Neal family, or whether we were merely its final proof. At all events, we starved, in the fine old sense of the word.

A depression, in its opening stages, may actually benefit the legal profession. Short money makes short tempers, and both make law-suits. But when men who have lent too freely finally sue and fore-close on everybody within reach, law offices become good places to catch up on reading. A woman wanting a divorce may find legal fees prohibitive in times of depression. Besides, depressions mean thin blankets; these combined with cold winter nights have effected many a reconciliation.

Not only was there the depression, but Dad detested one-party politics and felt compelled to take an active interest in Republican affairs, even though it cost him business in solidly Democratic territory. He always kept his clients' interests at heart instead of his own, and sometimes it was hard to watch him persuade hotheads to settle their differences out of court, in order to save their per-sonal relationships as well as money. The money saved consisted of court costs and lawyers' fees: fees which would have come in ever so handy filling the Neal bellies. But we were proud of our prin-ciples.

I reached the summer of my seventh year before becoming con-scious of family economics. It started gradually.

Elizabeth Porter walked up the road past our house early one Sunday morning. In response to my greeting, she asked, "Why haven't I seen you in Sunday School, Harry?"

Somewhere down the line I had been vaccinated with that pleas-ant lie they tell about George Washington and the cherry tree, and I replied quite honestly, "Mother says I can't go because I don't have any clothes to wear." That seems to have put an abrupt period to our remarks, for my next recollection is of her back, hurry-ing on toward town.

I went in the house, where Mother and Dad were still in bed, and bragged about telling the truth. There was an unnerving silence, and instead of commending me, Mother observed quietly that I should not have told Miss Porter that I did not have any good clothes to wear.

"But it was the truth, Mother; they say you're always supposed to tell the truth. . . ."

"Harry, there's something else they say," spoke Dad, also quietly. " 'Silence is golden.' Remember that."

In spite of the fact that we were doing without many things, it had not yet clearly dawned on me that we were desperately poor. The Sunday-morning incident must have aroused some vague misgivings, however, because a few weeks later, in midsummer of 1935, I asked Mother if we were rich. Unfortunately, I could not have picked a worse time.

The interview was something of a shock to me, and I remember the details plainly. It was late in a blazing summer morning, and since early hours Mother had been doing the family wash. Out in the yard a large iron kettle boiled over a fire of sticks which she had gathered the day before. Every now and then she would go up to poke the clothes with an old broomhandle. When I approached her she was on the porch scrubbing shirts on a corrugated washboard; it rested in one of two tubs filled with hand-drawn well water. She was using lye soap I had watched her make; the formula had been wrong and it always made her hands red and raw. A homemade dress was plastered to her body, almost as wet as the clothes she was wringing out.

All this, and up comes a grubby little savage who blurts, "Mother, are we rich?"

She wiped the sweat out of her eyes and said quite plainly, "No, we're not."

I was dumfounded. My question was not really a serious one, and I had expected only a smile and a yes and a pat on the back. My tongue was stiff in my throat.

"If we're not rich, then, what are we?"

Only then did she pause from her work. I watched her look off over the hill past the outhouse, sigh, and start scrubbing again.

"I guess we're poor, Harry."

There it was. Presently, when school came around, I noticed that I wore summer tennis shoes until the weather became quite chilly; convinced that every child in the room was watching my feet, I resorted to any excuse to keep them out of sight under my desk. I noticed that my lunches were of biscuits, because we couldn't afford "store-bought" bread. Other kids would take their sandwiches out of lunchboxes, open wrappers, and then begin to eat. I would reach inside my paper bag, sneak the biscuit out just in time to grab a fleeting bite, and then rush the offending biscuit back into the sack again. When we ran out of baking soda at home and my biscuits were flat and sour, I was convinced every child in school was laughing over it; I never considered that half of them might have troubles of their own. Many Orientals feel that public eating is indecent; when I see pictures of them covering their food with their hands, I have guilty memories of my unhappy grade-school days.

My clothes were homemade, and I became inordinately sensitive to the fact. I developed the mannerism of hugging my elbows, to hide holes in my sleeves. Fortunately I was for some years spared the awful suspicion of what had actually happened on all those mornings when Bill and I arose to a skimpy breakfast and our parents claimed that they had eaten "before you got up."

Finally, Dad was unable to keep up payments on our house, and we had to move to another, located in town. From there I often went to school empty-handed, with instructions to come home for lunch. Even today I flinch for Mother when I remember how sometimes she spent a whole morning gathering walnuts from nearby trees, and cracking a plateful of them for my lunch.

One snowy afternoon, we were completely out of kerosene for our cookstove, and practically out of food. I was given the family's bankroll, forty cents, and was sent after a gallon of kerosene, a package of dried beans, and something else which escapes me now. I put my hands into my pocket, closed my fingers about the money to make sure it was safe, and have no recollections beyond that point. When I reached the store, my money was gone. I felt a hot flush all over; wringing my hands, I ran back and forth over the block and a half I had carried the money.

I prayed, and cried, and poked through the slushy snow, but all to no avail. Finally, I got up nerve enough to go home, but Mother sent me back to look once again. I searched until night fell.

An old family letter of Mother's, dated April 16, 1936, had a pathetic paragraph:

"Our shortchange has not served to raise their [the children's] culinary standards. Yesterday they were telling what they would have if they had fifty dollars. Among the other unfestive things mentioned were 'wieners and good old mashed potatoes' finished off with a dessert of 'two hamburgers apiece.' That seemed so pitiful to me that I went off by myself and cried."

The next winter, Mrs. Priestly Jernigan encouraged me to play with her son Dan, who was in my grade at school. The first time I was invited to lunch there, Mother gave me a serious talk about table manners, about not bossing the other little boy around, and about thanking people for things. I came home fairly bursting with news. They had the most wonderful meal anyone could possibly imagine.

"They had pork and salad and butterbeans and candied potatoes and string beans and—oh!—just everything. And they had ice cream and cake. It was a dinner fit for a king!"

Late that night I heard my name in the soft murmur behind Mother and Dad's door. Slipping out of bed I crept closer and heard Dad say, "My guess is the little urchin ate a stomachful, talking all the time."

Mother: "I wonder how deeply he betrayed us. . . ."

The only recollections I have of the third grade are of Miss Ray telling me not to talk so much, and of resurrecting my old song about Sonja Henie. I went to Miss Adams, whom I still thought as pretty as ever, and tried to curry favor by asking if she would write the song down for me properly. She told me to come to her office after school and all day I shivered with pleasure at the prospect of being that close to her, and alone.

After she wrote out the song we had a talk. Either I had been showing signs of musical aptitude which I do not now remember, or she was apprehensive about my romantic notions concerning her and wished to turn them aside. At all events, she announced that arrangements had been made for me to have piano lessons with a local teacher, Miss May Corum. She understood that we had no money; the lessons were to be free, and I was to be given access to school pianos for practice.

I ran all the way home.

"YOU MUST LEAVE THIS TOWN"

Mother's reaction was somewhat dampening; there were questions: Who said I was going to study piano? How could we pay for lessons? A piano? Sheet music? These matters I disposed of between gasps of breath, but finally came a question to which I had no answer.

"Even if your piano lessons are free, Bill will have to have lessons, too. How on earth can we pay for his?"

It was a telling point. There was healthy competition between us boys, and it was unbreakable family law that what one of us had, the other had. I often thought the chief application of this law was to buy Bill a pair of pants, and give them to me when he had worn them out. But sometimes I was unreasonable about it myself. Mother tells that when we were quite small, she heard me burst out crying during breakfast one morning. And what was wrong?

"Billy ate one biscuit more than I did."

"Well, now, don't cry; I'll just get you another one."

The volume of howls rose perceptibly and she was just able to understand my cry, "But I *can't* eat another one!"

The piano lesson problem was solved by letting both of us study. However, my parents refused free tuition, feeling it was charity. Bill, Mother and I all worked for Miss Corum to pay for the lessons.

In spite of all our fuss about problems, we were overlooking the one matter of lifetime significance: I was nearly nine years old, and my musical training was beginning three years too late. It usually requires about 10,000 hours' practice to acquire a pianistic technique of professional caliber; obviously this apprenticeship should begin at the earliest possible moment if one's artistic equipment is to be acquired before habits harden and the body matures. For this reason concert artists usually come from families, or cultural environments, which discover and encourage their talents in the preschool age.

31

Starting lessons at the age of nine need not in itself be a serious handicap to learning the piano. But it was for me, because it reflected the fact that my family knew nothing about music, and they knew few people who did. My home town was a wonderfully friendly place, but it was not enriched by any great cultural tradition.

Paris, Tennessee, was critically examined during the Civil War by Captain Charles Nott of the Union Army, who campaigned through this part of Tennessee. His observations were published in a small volume entitled *Sketches of the War,* and are well worth reading.

He was amazed to see the populace living on a diet of pork and corn pone; often there were four pork dishes during a single meal. His junior officers could never accustom themselves to asking some charming local belle a gallant question, and waiting while she spat out a stream of tobacco juice before replying. Perhaps we can forgive his conclusion: that the Southerners' "hot blood"—and indeed the whole war itself—must have been caused by bad cooking and too much tobacco!

After his first visit to Paris, he wrote the following:

"They are a strange people, these gay Parisians, full of inconsistencies and all sorts of incongruous traits. They neither smile nor frown, nor agree nor disagree; but have a vague stupid look of frightened wonder, as though we were dangerous serpents escaped from a travelling menagerie, which they can see for nothing at the risk of being swallowed alive. They are not a musical people; you never hear a boy whistle, or a girl singing at her work; they are not liberally educated, and schoolmasters are few. Yet in half the houses you will find pianos, and half the women play by note."

Almost every little girl in the South can tinkle on a piano, but this is a social, rather than a cultural phenomenon. Children study music to acquire a social grace rather than artistic understanding. As a result an army of teachers annoy their pupils with such masterpieces as "It's a Gum Drop Tree," in grade school, until they are finally graduated from high school playing "Invitation to the Dance" twice too slow. At least half of each year is spent in preparation for a socio-musical calamity rather grandly known as the "annual spring recital." These recitals lose any proper function as by-products of musical study, and become its only purpose. Continual public performance misleads parents into thinking their investment has all been worth while, but the continually interrupted music study—with undue stress laid on worthless little pieces which have no inspirational value—usually succeeds in killing whatever inclination the children originally had toward music.

Boys (naturally more spunky than girls) usually get a bellyful and throw the whole thing up after three or four seasons. The rest get out of school unable to play serious music worth a hoot, though that is what they have devoted their entire study to for years. Almost all private music teachers concentrate on performance alone (for this is what shows up in recitals), and virtually ignore sight-reading and music appreciation. Therefore the average child can neither play nor understand good music, and isn't able to sight-read well enough to play much popular music. The usual result is for young people to give up music completely after graduating from high school; their parents' investment is wasted, but worse, they live and die without suspecting the sublime truth of Beethoven.

Just as I began to study the piano, my personality problems took a more serious turn. If money does talk, it was saying good-bye to us, and I became increasingly sensitive about it.

People are quite different humans with money than they are without it; some show up better, some worse. At the age of nine I tried to answer the problem of my inferiority complex by deciding that I was a Superior Being. To this pleasant fantasy I applied myself with great diligence.

Naturally, I got everything backwards.

I discovered that I could excel in schoolwork and in music without working overly hard. No one forced me to do otherwise, and it became a matter of honor for me to get by with as little work as humanly possible; my great daily glory was in walking home without the burden of homework books carried by my fellow students. Such airs threatened to make it impossible for me to reach the very superiority I sought.

In my twelfth year, I added a new wrinkle: I accused my fellow seventh-graders of being childish, which may have been correct; however I incorrectly assumed that stating the fact made me mature. How well I remember Miss Wyman, my teacher, asking if I were going to the carnival that night. There was nothing in this world that I wanted more, but all the other children were going, so I replied that it was childish to enjoy such things and I had gotten over it long before. Miss Wyman quietly threw me a curve by mentioning that she still liked carnivals very much. I was quite lost for a reply.

I developed exhibitionism, and started misbehaving in class; conduct grades became one matter over which I had no control. How grateful I was when they began issuing report cards every six weeks instead of every month! I was grateful because my conduct grades were always "C," and Mother always impressed it on me that they should be "A"; her impressions being made firmly with a strap on my backside.

Perhaps my delusions of superiority did have a few good effects. Though I would not study in school, I wanted to know things; this was due partly to a very real curiosity, and partly to the vain pleasure of confounding my friends with strange bits of knowledge. I undertook great projects to read entire sets of encyclopedias (unfinished), and to read enormous dictionaries (unfinished).

Somewhere I ran across Dr. Johnson's remark about a man's books being the key to his character. Therefore, at the age of twelve I was careful to be seen by my classmates reading such books as *Quo Vadis* and *Ben Hur*. These, however, I finished promptly; unwittingly I had stumbled on the great truth that "good" books are so called simply because they are too good to put down until finished.

When I started spending my afternoons in the Paris public library I was on the right track. Without guidance, much of my time was wasted on the paltry stuff classed as "children's books," but the musty little library was small enough for an active boy to scour inch by inch, and I often came home with magical books which changed my life. The library shelves had tags identifying book categories. In the summer of 1940 I asked the librarian what the sign marked "Psychology" meant.

"Oh, don't bother with that, Harry. It's too far advanced for you."

It was all the invitation I needed. That afternoon I carried home the smallest book on the shelf: a thin, brown, paperbacked little bombshell entitled *Principles of Human Behavior*. I lay down in the back yard and read it from cover to cover. For the first time in my life, I saw the term "inferiority complex." I read how a sensitive person might assume a "defense mechanism" in the form of an artificial "superiority complex."

For a long time my public conduct had been completely out of control. I made faces, talked too loud, made senseless remarks, and was—to employ a term overused in my youth—"smart-alecky." The reproaches of my parents were nothing compared to those I heaped upon myself, but in spite of all my resolutions, some demon seemed to take hold of me in public, where my actions were designed only to humiliate me and those who loved me. Now, at last, I understood that Harry Neal, the cocksure show-off, was simply a mask which I—and all the other little boys like me—assumed just to keep people from knowing how scared we were.

I had achieved my first bit of self-awareness, and that was good. On the other hand, a little knowledge was no better for me than it is for ordinary people, and the discovery that I had a soul, and that it was sensitive, deep and mysterious, was one of dubious value.

Rather than curing my troubles, I had stumbled upon one supreme way to feel superior to all mere mortals. I was more *sensitive* than they. I could suffer. And be tragic. And tormented. And noble. I could take long walks, and indeed I did everything but wander over the moors crying, "Heathcliff!"

All of this introspection led to one genuine and sincere personal crisis, which lasted throughout my teens.

Both my grandfathers were lay ministers, my mother a Sunday School teacher, and the local culture strongly religious. Somewhere in my readings I ran across those famous words of the agnostic to his Christian friend, "If I believed what you *say* you believe, I would crawl on my hands and knees over a bed of red hot coals to tell everyone in the world." The challenge was unavoidable: if I believed what I had been taught, I would have no alternative but to forsake everything else in the world for it, for what else could be important?

The decision was made for me to become a minister; soon afterward a desire to be honest caused me to undertake a critical examination of my own thinking for the first time in my life.

It became my custom to visit a different church each Sunday, seeking as many views as possible. After a few weeks I began to suspect that one might sit through most sermons without having his thoughts disturbed in the least. I bought a book on comparative religion, and was amazed to discover that ideas I had always believed to be only 2,000 years old had occurred to others long before. Indeed, it seemed that every time wise men sat down by the banks of a river to think, they arrived at very much the same conclusions about Man's relation to God and to his fellow creatures.

It did not ease my perplexity to discover that God's servants were only men. I had always thought ministers were each and every one divinely consecrated persons, and was sure that every word they spoke was absolutely dedicated to Truth. Away from home one Sunday morning, I marveled to hear a preacher—renowned over the entire South—describe one of his early experiences: in an Arkansas mining town he had attempted to convert a miner, who felt that accepting Christ was too easy a price to pay for the marvelous benefits of life hereafter. On visiting the mines, the minister complained of the gloomy underground tunnels, and asked this miner how he could get outside.

"Just step in that lift, sir, and press the button."

"What? Do you mean that all I have to do to leave this dismal chamber, and rise to the beauty of the birds, and the flowers, and the sun and the sky and the glorious world outside—is just to press a button? I don't believe you; *it's too easy!*"

I marveled at the man's wisdom and his ability to turn a chance situation to his advantage. Actually, he was turning more to his advantage than I thought.

On a following Sunday I returned to my home church. Looking down from the choir loft that morning, I heard my own minister wind up to tell of one of *his* experiences in a *Kentucky* mining town. My incredulous ears heard him describe a miner who believed salvation was all "too easy." In an instant the truth flashed over me. Somewhere—perhaps in the last issue of a religious periodical—these two men had read a made-to-order anecdote and incorporated it into their sermons. I had no quarrel with that, for it was a good story and made an excellent point. However, common honesty denied any reason but vanity for each of them to claim it as one of his personal master strokes.

At any rate, my minister had not the originality to change one adjective or preposition in the story. By the time he got to the birds and the flowers and the glorious et cetera, I was a profoundly disturbed young man.

My prayers became more and more agitated, as I became conscious that one of my chief motivations was simply a fear of hell. I detected that I was just trying to make a swap: seventy years here, for eternity There. It was very nearly a business transaction, rather than a spiritual matter, and if I could not fool myself, it seemed unlikely that I should fool God. I began to see that there was vanity in my desire to preach. I wished to appear wise, and have people marvel while I told them how to live. Finally I reached the bitter decision that I was unfit to preach.

At the time I was not mature enough to find chinks in any portion of my religious beliefs without doubting the whole structure. A few years passed in which I was unable even to believe in God. This is not to say that I disbelieved, but rather that I refused to allow myself to believe in anything unless I had more than hearsay evidence to go on. My friends insisted that, with my classing the Bible as hearsay, I had cut myself off from any means of reaching the Truth: they rather underestimated God, for He reaches different people in different ways. He made me become a musician—and no serious man can approach the sanctity of Beethoven's slow movements without in some sense getting on his knees to do so.

Because of God I found music, and through music I found God.

Nevertheless, my spiritual struggles were agonizing, and I have since had little patience with men who approached the problem without due gravity. Last May my wife and I played for a church-sponsored college in nearby Jackson, Tennessee. A ministerial student was describing his little mission church to me; finally he observed, "Oh, yes, I'm very interested in music." Thinking I would be pleased by our common interest, he added, "I came here to study trumpet, but they had no trumpet teacher, so I took up the ministry instead."

The Lord moves in mysterious ways, indeed!

Regardless of all ignorance, laziness and false ideas, I was achieving a sense of personal destiny, and trying to reach serious decisions about life. More and more I came to find in music an outlet which answered some need I did not yet understand.

Up to this time I had been content to follow the local herd, plumbing the depths of musical mediocrity. Now I began to take music more seriously, and the amount of my practice improved, if its quality did not. Practicing music quickly and efficiently is a highly developed art, and is quite different from "playing" the piano; all I knew to do with my new enthusiasm was to spend more time "playing" my music.

I had the idea that music expresses emotions. Languishing with a sentimental longing for a preacher's daughter who lived across the street, I would arrange all my music in an order which told a "story." A certain "clickety-clack" piece might represent me galloping along on a horse; a slow section of the Reinhold *Impromptu* allowed me to discover her—unconscious—beside the road and woo her back to life (For what it is worth, I discovered her by noticing her long hair, which tumbled out across the road. Those tresses would have had to be nine feet long in order to reach as far as I imagined, but it *was* a delicious thought!); the razzle-tazzle finale was me doing great battles in her behalf, and we finally returned to the ever-present Reinhold *Impromptu*, where she and I declared mutual love, etc., etc., forever. This all seemed very plain to me, and I would beat these pieces out by the day, hoping that she would hear them, be overwhelmed, and come across the street to say that she loved me.

Apparently I did not play loudly enough. She never came.

All the while I was making a certain provincial mark for myself, though little of it had any real significance. I won various contests, played in numerous recitals, and generally undistinguished myself. Lacking musicianship, I "interpreted" Paderewski's *Minuet*, for instance, simply by imitating his recording of that work (which I loved) just as exactly as possible. After playing it in a concert in Memphis, some ancient man (described to me as "*very important*") took my arm in the way that such men do, declaring to all and sundry that he had "heard Paderewski play that piece many times, and this boy sounds just exactly like him!"

A parrot might repeat "e=mc²," but he's no Einstein.

I was thirteen years old, and had never heard a serious concert. We did not own a phonograph, or a single record. We had possessed a radio for only two years, and I was as yet unaware of good music on the air. I was just another of those talented small-town children who have not the vaguest idea what is meant when people refer to music as an art.

At this point a local lady, Miss Nelle Ketchum, decided to bring culture to our fair city, and financed a concert series here. It was fated for an early death; people usually wish to be entertained— not improved. A group of local amateurs was presenting an eight-piano program, and Miss Ketchum thought it might fit in nicely to have a good, professional two-piano team for her first concert. Instead the reaction was, "Why should I pay a dollar to hear only two pianos when I can pay fifty cents and hear eight?"

I could not afford tickets, but Miss Nelle, bless her heart, let me in to every concert as an usher. Only those who love music as something a little greater than life can know how my parched soul drank up that first concert. I had no idea what they were playing, what it meant, or whether they played well or badly. I had no idea what to listen for in music, except "the tune"; later I was to learn that listening to music for melody alone is somewhat like reading the Bible for its story—but at the time I was satisfied.

That night a skinny little boy—dressed in his only good suit— became a future concert pianist.

The concert artist cannot help wondering, sometimes, if his life is really worth what it costs him. He lives under an exacting schedule; his sleep is irregular and there is never enough of it; there are countless personal demands made on him in each town he visits; it is almost impossible for him to get sufficient practice; for months he takes every meal in a different restaurant; he spends every night on a different bed. No matter how gregarious, he suffers great loneliness in the midst of multitudes.

The deepest cut of all is that almost no one seems to understand him, or what he is trying to do. He has one experience at the concert hall, and his listeners have another; almost never does anyone come backstage to compliment him for what *he* felt to be the high point of the evening. The usual pattern is for him to give one of the most gratifying performances of his career, only to have some plump old matron come back and congratulate him for a silly encore he was half ashamed to play.

Sometimes the temptation is strong to relax one's artistic standards: "I am so tired; this is such a small town—they will understand nothing anyway—why should I make such an effort? Why should I tear my soul out for them?"

When I begin to feel discouraged, I like to remember that Paris, Tennessee, was a mere $100 engagement Francis Hall and Jerome Rappaport picked up because they happened to be playing nearby. We were perhaps their smallest town, their smallest fee; by purely materialistic standards they might have been justified had they chosen to give us their smallest effort. Instead, that night they communicated something which revolutionized my entire life.

Whenever I face a disappointingly small crowd in some provincial little town, I like to imagine that somewhere on the back row is another skinny little boy—dressed in his only good suit—who was sneaked in because he could not afford the price of a ticket. No matter what artistic disappointments I may have had, it is always easy to pour out my soul, not for the local dilettante who *claims* to understand—but for the little boy who may one day *come* to understand.

The handing down of this artistic legacy from one musical soul to another is very like being

> blessed by a man
> who was blessed by a man
> who was blessed by a man
> who was blessed by a
> Carpenter.

The question became, "Do I have enough talent to become a concert pianist?"

I was as ignorant as a poor boy can be. I had begun to worry about intangibles and was terrified to discover that all my tentacles of inquiry were waving hopelessly in the abyss of "I don't know."

I asked Miss May, my teacher, and she replied that a concert career was out of the question. Actually, she gave me the right answer; all odds are against any given child's ever becoming a concert artist. However, I was unsympathetic to Miss May's denial of my dream, and at that point I became her future ex-pupil. Many people did encourage me, but I knew they were unqualified, and would say anything to be nice to an ambitious little boy.

My brother Bill had an inspiration. We had just acquired a phonograph, and he bought the Horowitz-Toscanini recording of Tchaikovsky's *Concerto in B-flat minor.*

"Do you think you can play like that?" he asked.

Surprisingly, the record failed to discourage me, for technical difficulties vanish under an artist's fingers, and nothing is left but music. Everything Horowitz did sounded so natural and effortless that I actually supposed the music was easy. Oh, to be thirteen again, and able—without effort—to surpass the greatest of pianists!

Dad tried to keep my feet on the ground by cautioning me not to be deceived by apparent ease on the part of a performer. He admitted no knowledge of music, but reminded me that "ignorant country audiences may like the baseball player who flails the air, races back and forth, and is constantly making catches which seem impossible. A professional scout," he said, "looks for the man who is always in place, and plays his position with unassuming ease."

Mother didn't know what to tell me except to say that if I had enough talent to become a concert artist, I would undoubtedly practice all day long every day, on my own initiative.

Some children do, but generally speaking this is just a popular fairy tale. There is no known connection between musical talent and the desire to work. We come into this world as completely undisciplined organisms, and resist every encroachment upon our freedom—whether it is learning not to draw on the living-room wall, or (later in life) learning to keep our mouths shut. I know many concert pianists, and almost every one of them had to have his bottom beaten before he would keep it on a piano stool. Nobody beat my bottom, and what I gained on one end I lost on the other. Soon, I had acquired the habit of both mental and physical laziness.

Almost every hamlet in the country boasts of men who were Almost Big Time. It is surprising how many of these men actually did have the makings of high-powered lawyers, doctors, or whatever. Very often their failure to achieve spectacular success can be traced back to just one wrong decision, one mistake, one weakness, or perhaps one piece of bad luck.

At the age of fourteen I had one piece of *good* luck: just before it was forever too late, someone pointed my nose in the right direction.

The successful man is tempted to say there is no such thing as luck; failures often try to blame everything on luck. Personally, I can claim no credit for the good break of my fourteenth year; it is a healthily sobering thought that many of the frustrated musicians I meet while we are on tour might have become more successful performers than I if only they had received good advice before it was too late.

Into all the confusion of my musical ambitions came the first professional artist I ever knew. Howard Rothschild was a sensitive and sophisticated artist who joined the United States Army immediately after Pearl Harbor and America's entry into World War II. For a short time he was stationed at Camp Tyson, a barrage-balloon training center just outside of Paris, Tennessee.

Howard came to Miss May, my teacher, to ask if he might use her piano for practice on his days off. She graciously opened her home to him and also asked him to hear me play, thereby giving my life a turning point for which I shall always be grateful. Howard gave me the enlightened encouragement which I so desperately needed. Just after my fourteenth birthday, he delivered the lecture which finally gave some direction and purpose to my musical life.

He was blunt. "Harry, you probably are musical enough to become a concert artist, but it is terribly late in your life, as a pianist's development goes. If you ever expect to make the grade, you must leave this town soon, go to a metropolitan teacher, listen to worlds of music, and work your fingers to the bone. You should be able to do it, but for heaven's sake, don't be so cocky; there are children your age already playing concerti with orchestras."

He said just the right thing at just the right time in my life, and I shall be eternally indebted to him for it. I was encouraged, determined, and seriously troubled by my musical failings. His remarks were made at 3:15 in the afternoon of May 16, 1942; a new day in my life had begun.

        June 6, 1942   *Sydney, Australia*

My dear Allison,

I have just heard [the broadcast of] your playing in the D minor concerto of Mendelssohn. I am delighted. I'm sure I won't "spoil" you if I say that the performance was one of the freshest, happiest, most naturally musical I have heard for years. Your technique is exceptional, but I never for a moment thought of technique, while this felicitous music came rippling from your fingers. . . . Now, my dear Allison, I am not in the habit of using superlative language about young artists. But I know that you will not ever grow over-confident. Take care of the rare talent that, by the grace of the gods, is in you. It is precious. You have been chosen as the vessel and safeguard of this genius. Treasure it with pride and love and modesty. You are a very fortunate girl, and—I am sure—very happy in your gifts.

                                    Yours sincerely,

                                    Neville Cardus *

Your playing was so happy—always play for and from happiness.

A year went by before my parents could scrape together enough money for me to take piano lessons away from Paris.

In the meantime, there was nothing for me to do but continue my studies here. I was all boy, and still had no idea what it meant to concentrate on the piano, or anything else. Instead, I dabbled in every possible school activity, got into all kinds of trouble, and started developing the first of those wild schemes which the family tolerantly referred to as my "brainstorms."

Trying to broaden my musical knowledge, I spent much time in the high school band. Its chief contribution to my life, however, was to let me see football games for nothing. If only our student body had applied the ferocity to its studies that it did to those football games! Savage emotions were about all we could muster,

---

* Neville Cardus, one of Europe's distinguished musical critics, writes for a noted English paper, *The Manchester Guardian.* He spent the war years in Australia.

though, for my only recollections of the games are of those funereal rides home. At that age I was convinced that for the rest of my life I would be pointed out to strangers as the fellow who went to "that school Mayfield licked 50 to 7 back in '42."

Football trips were not the only ones which ended gloomily. My parents scraped up enough money to buy me a new coat and send me 300 miles to hear my first great pianist—Rachmaninoff—in Knoxville. After I reached Knoxville, he canceled the concert. I was one heartbroken boy.

Mostly, though, the year was packed with good, noisy boyhood. I paid for it dearly later on, but somehow I have never begrudged myself that last careless year. I didn't learn much about the piano, but my education was not totally neglected.

Although technically a town boy, I bought a pig and joined the 4-H Club on the strength of it. We couldn't afford commercial feed, so I collected slop from local restaurants every day after school. Some neighbors were annoyed by the smell and reported me to the police for violating a city no-animal ordinance, but I loved Junior (my pig) and elected to fight it out. Luck came to my aid, for we soon discovered that the city limits passed right through our back yard; I might be a city boy, but Junior was a county pig, beyond the reach of local law. I drank the cup of triumph.

One of my less useful projects was to read literature about judo. It was my favorite boast that I knew six different ways to kill a man with only one blow. Perhaps with a brickbat I might have.

Along about then I had my first date—and a blind one at that. The occasion was a watermelon feast at the Tennessee River, some twenty miles away. The watermelons were not very exciting, but our chaperone was kind enough to ride in the cab of the truck while we innocent young things enjoyed an incredibly slow hay ride to and from the river.

This was all fine, except that my date and I sat primly and discussed intellectual matters the full distance of both trips. We were the only couple so employed, and keenly aware of it. To make matters worse, my adored little preacher's daughter was enjoying a particularly amorous evening with somebody else, just over my right shoulder. "Youth is like spring, an overpraised season. . . ."

One of my activities was later to pay good dividends for the time it took away from music. Paris boasted an excellent dramatics teacher, and I discovered a professional talent for the spoken word. As you might suppose, I felt pretty good about it. My dramatics teacher, Mrs. Krider, finally told me a story:

"A man saw that his two daughters were becoming conceited. He sat down with them, holding a balloon in one hand, and described to them a young lady who met with successes everywhere she went. At each new success, the man would tell how her head got bigger, and then gave a great puff on his balloon. Finally, as the balloon was about to burst, his daughters drew away from it. 'Yes!' he cried. 'That's what all her friends did, and that's what all *your* friends are doing!' "

I thought it was a fine story, and that the young girls were stupid to be so conceited. Three years passed before I realized that those words had been meant for me. In some ways my mentality was not all that I thought.

Late in my freshman year at high school, I read that Beethoven had quit his lessons with Haydn because he'd discovered uncorrected mistakes in his copybook.

It forced me to realize that for years I too had been getting away with sloppy work at school and in music. Now I was brought up short with the question, "If my teachers let me get away with foolishness which even *I* can see, how many things must be wrong that I don't even know about?" A whole year had been wasted remembering only the convenient side of what Howard Rothschild had told me: that I "should" be able to make the grade as a pianist. Now I remembered that he also told me to seek artist teachers, if I ever expected to become an artist myself. My fifteenth birthday was approaching, and I knew something would have to be done.

A slight improvement in Neal finances permitted my parents to send me away for weekly piano lessons during the following summer. It was a thousand miles to New York; Dad could afford to send me only twenty-two miles up the highway to a teacher at a small college in Murray, Kentucky. Their comparative mileages may also have suggested the artistic distances involved, but at least my inertia was broken.

I had left my womb of complacency, and the first step in my move from Paris, Tennessee, had begun.

It was a hot June morning in Murray, Kentucky, when I arrived at the State Teachers College for my first piano lesson. Russell Baldwin, my new teacher, listened silently as I banged out a Beethoven sonata, a Chopin scherzo, and lacerated Mozart's *Fantasy in D minor.*

My ignorance was a merciful thing for me, if not for him; I had no idea how bad it was. Before him stood the canvas of my artistic awareness, and it was completely bare, except for a few childish scribblings across the bottom edge. For the first time in my life, someone placed a brush in the paint-pot of musical integrity, and dabbed a clear spot of color on my vacant consciousness.

"I don't like your Mozart style," he commented with heroic restraint.

Rumbling home in the tired little bus that afternoon, I pondered over his remark. Style? What did he mean? I had always supposed that music was music, no matter who wrote it. Was he suggesting that each composer wrote differently, and had to be played in a different manner? How terrible! How would you ever keep up with it all? The next week he confounded me by correcting mistakes in the printed music. I rushed home breathless with excitement. "Mother! Mother! He actually knows as much as the composer! He even knows *harmony,* too!"

There was no telling where these disturbing new thoughts might come from. Waiting for my lesson one day, I pulled a mimeographed sheet out of the wastepaper basket. It quoted some woman somewhere as saying that young people should learn to read music as readily as a newspaper. I was amazed at such a conception. Up until that time I had thought it quite normal for everyone to pick out music, note by note, just as I did. But now it seemed that a musician should be able to play works off, the very first time he saw them! It was a terrifying thought.

Looking back, I can see that Russell Baldwin made a few mistakes with me. Once we listened to a record by a well-known pianist, and he pointed out several wrong notes in it. I, who should have heard of nothing but perfectionism, learned that prominent artists are sometimes guilty of bad playing. It was very convenient for me to slip back a notch or two toward complacency, and feel that my mistakes were not too great a crime after all.

Usually, however, he showed a great flair for handling young Neal. I was not too far removed from the cops-and-robbers stage (little boys want adventure in their music as well as their books), so it was purely elementary psychology for him to introduce me to the music of Liszt. It has a wild flamboyance which could appeal to my sense of drama, and force me to develop technique at the same time.

But the key to Baldwin's effect on my life ran more deeply than that: he had the power to arouse my dormant passion for music.

"Harry, I want you to study Liszt's *Second Hungarian Rhapsody* for next week. You know, I've played this piece for years, but I envy you this opportunity to study it for the first time. There's a wonderful experience ahead of you; it's like falling in love—never again in later life can you recapture that *first time*."

What exciting words for an eager young mind! Suddenly a whole new world of experience opened up before me. I had my first glimpses of the exultation one feels in discovering great new music. Wondering what it was that Baldwin envied, I began for the first time to examine my reactions to music, to notice what excited me and to try to understand why. I began to comprehend music as a great emotional force.

Week after week, Baldwin hacked away at my ignorance, until little speckles of knowledge began to appear on the bare canvas of my artistic consciousness. At the time, I could sense no pattern to them, and the effect on me was one of confusion. It would remain for someone else to fill in the reaches between these splashes of color, and weld them into an artistic whole.

But, late one August morning, Russell Baldwin gave me what I so desperately needed. He filled in one figure on my canvas clearly enough that it made complete sense even to me. High in the upper-right-hand corner of my picture-to-be he painted a beautiful guiding star for me to follow. I had asked, hesitantly, about the concert stage.

"Sure," he mused. "You'd have to work like the dickens, but you might make it. The problem for you is that I'm really not the teacher for you. Nobody around here is. And you don't have the money to afford the kind of teacher you need." I was hanging on every word. "What to do . . . what to do . . ." he mumbled, reaching for another cigarette.

It took him fully three or four years to light that cigarette and blow out his match. "Harry, there's a school in Philadelphia called the Curtis Institute of Music. It's small—maybe a hundred and fifty students—but it's one of the best conservatories in the world. They specialize in child prodigies, and nobody pays a cent to go there. The world's great players teach at Curtis, and some of them don't teach anywhere else. They have Primrose, Piatigorsky, Kincaid, Zimbalist, Salzedo—and Serkin teaches piano. He's probably my favorite pianist. They don't take students except by competitive audition, so you finish up high school and go try out for Curtis. "That's the best thing I can tell you."

For once in my life I moved with decision. It was obvious to me that I could not study piano in Paris again, and that I must move on beyond even Murray as quickly as possible. In the meantime, I decided to finish high school at the college demonstration school in Murray.

The college training school had smaller classes and better qualified teachers than our high school in Paris, and when fall came I enrolled as a student there. Baldwin soon left Murray, and I continued my piano lessons with Mr. Clair McGavern.

Few things are completely black or white. I was a curious mixture of hard work and slothfulness. In spite of all my energy and ambition, I had a great aversion to work. I put everything off as long as possible, and always counted on learning things in a blaze of study at the last minute. Educational standards are so low that every child has done this, and many are the English courses crammed the night before, and class plays memorized at dress rehearsal. Even while I was doing it, I used to wonder how much might be accomplished if one only had the character to sustain these efforts. The day was not too far distant when I would learn the answer to that question, and pay a bitter price for the cure to my laziness.

On the other hand, I was capable of great energy, and engaged in every imaginable school activity. My determination to get to Curtis as soon as possible drove me to finish up my remaining three years' high school work in the next two calendar years. The spring before graduation, I applied eagerly for my audition in Philadelphia. With their reply, my world tumbled down, for the Curtis Institute notified me that there were no vacancies in their piano class, and that there would be no auditions that year. How on earth could I ever get the education I wanted? For that matter, without their expert opinions, how could I be absolutely certain that I wasn't just kidding myself about becoming a pianist?

Two weeks later, I saw a poster advertising the National Music Camp at Interlochen, Michigan. My eyes froze on the camp's avowed purpose: "To answer the question, 'Does my child have enough talent to make music a career?'"

Dad agreed to finance the longest and most important trip I had ever made: a summer at the National Music Camp. This, however, would not leave him enough money to send me to a college away from home in the fall. It would be necessary that I enroll at Murray.

I agreed eagerly. I was seventeen years old.

The girl was now a young woman of seventeen.

One last time—she told herself—while the family is out of the house and away. She sat down at the old, familiar keyboard. The voices of her parents had faded, the reporters had vanished, the excitement was gone. How do you touch a piano for the last time?

Here, in this room, she had battled day and night as far back as memory could carry her. Here, long ago, she had bitten her hands and arms in a fury over their reluctance to master the Saint-Saëns G minor Concerto octaves. Here, six months ago, she prepared for the greatest tour of Australia ever attempted by an artist her age. Only ten days ago she was practicing here when the reporters rang up to say that Eugene Ormandy had returned to America and arranged a special scholarship for her to study at the famed Curtis Institute of Music.

Lord Gowrie, Governor-General of Australia, had personally cut through all wartime red tape to arrange her immediate passage to America as a special guest of the Swedish-American Steamship

*Line. In a few minutes she would leave this house on the longest
and most meaningful journey she had ever taken. All the life, and
tears, and love which she would leave with this piano!*

Perhaps, just one last time . . .

At the National Music Camp, my musical horizons broadened
suddenly. Maynard Klein, my choir director, made every work
come alive. I had always thought the object of music was to be
"pretty," and I shall never forget my shock one morning while we
worked on the Fauré *Requiem.*

"No! No! No!" he was angry. "I want an ugly sound from you
people—not that pretty Sunday School tone you've been singing
with! This is the *Dies Irae*—the Day of Wrath!—when God visits
all his fury on those who have defied Him.

"I want you," he flung out the words, "to give me a sound which
will make my blood run cold!"

I was working to help pay for my tuition at Interlochen. Walking to my job after choir rehearsal each morning, I became attracted by a kindly, bald-headed old man who spent his days
basking in the sun, and listening to orchestra rehearsals in the huge
outdoor bowl. His bright eyes always smiled a greeting, so one day
I paused to chat.

"Do you mind if I sit with you, sir?"

"Certainly not; in fact, I recommend it. It takes no more time to
fish with a smart man than a dumb one."

He was full of so many cogent observations about music and art
that I came back many times. After about three of our chats,
someone told me that he was Thaddeus P. Giddings, known as the
father of American public school music. At our next meeting I said
to him, "Mr. Giddings, why didn't you tell me who you were?"

"My dear boy, I was not vain enough to consider it interesting
conversation. You, on the other hand, had neither civility nor
curiosity enough to ask. The incivility I excuse; the lack of curiosity
I do not. Curiosity, you must learn, is the only sure sign of an active
mind."

Old age was a lonely time for Thaddeus Giddings. He was largely
overlooked there at camp, and sometimes I like to imagine that
my wide-eyed hero worship may have made my visits as pleasant

for him as they were exciting to me. His was the first penetratingly skeptical mind I had met on intimate ground. Often we sat below the tall pines, scarcely exchanging a word. Now and again Mr. Giddings would turn to me with an observation or answer to some question, but mostly we warmed ourselves sleepily in the sunlight, the music, and one another's company. Secretly I came to resent the intrusion of other students, who sometimes joined us.

Once while away from the music buildings he suddenly exclaimed, "How dreadful!" His goatee bristled, and four of us campers quailed. "What a frightful *vibrato!* Her voice is quivering like a hootchy-kootchy dancer. There—do you hear it?"

"Oh, yes!" chorused the others, while I strained my ears, hearing nothing. He looked over his spectacles.

"And you, Harry?"

"Gosh, I don't hear anything at all."

"Hm. Stupid, but honest. Don't worry, these others are just stupid and dishonest; they didn't hear anything either."

Later, he comforted me. "You've hardly ever played on a piano that was in tune; how can you expect suddenly to understand niceties of pitch variation?"

"That's right, sir. I always thought a nice, jangly, out-of-tune note was much prettier than one that was just tuned. Tuned notes are so pale and flat sounding."

"Boy," he chuckled, "you warm my old bones. But let me tell you something. You've got to learn to hear these things. If you ever expect to do anything in this world, you'll have to develop your powers of observation. Life depends on little things, and you never know which little thing you see or hear will prove to be terribly important later on. You must notice absolutely *everything.*"

After listening to me play one day, he delivered himself of a lecture.

"Harry, you've got good instincts, but very little knowledge— very little technical equipment. You play musically, but you don't know why or how; you just try to *feel* the music, and hope something will come out. Well, sometimes it does, but that's not enough. You've got to know objectively what you are doing at every moment!

"Most people quote only the words, 'Poetry is a spontaneous

overflow of powerful emotion,' and stop there, leaving off the most important phrase of all: 'recollected in tranquility.' You can't expect to create anything artistic on emotion alone. Haven't you ever waked up some morning and winced to read a love letter you'd written the night before?" (How he hit home then!) "There's a vast difference between feeling an emotion yourself and making other people feel it. You need to be a thinker as well as a feeler!"

All I could understand was that he was not approving of my playing. "I guess it's pretty hopeless," I mumbled.

"Oh, goodness, you *are* a fool," he snapped. "It would be hopeless if you couldn't feel, because that's something nobody can teach you; but even *you*, ninny, can learn to think!"

Like Russell Baldwin two summers before, he chipped away at my ignorance and complacence. There at Interlochen I was for the first time in my life studying with an artist teacher, Dorsey Whittington, of the Birmingham Conservatory of Music in Alabama; between him and Giddings, I began to acquire some real bits and pieces of a musical background. But still, they seemed to have no relation, and I could sense no pattern to it all. Dr. Whittington commented that my playing of a certain phrase was "breathless," and I asked Giddings about it. By answer he made a beautiful statement which is as vivid and important to me today as it was when I first heard him say it: "Every instrumentalist tries to imitate the human voice in melodic phrasing." Going on, he added, "At the piano, you must take a breath at the end of a phrase, just as though you were singing it. Usually, ninny, you do it instinctively, but you've got to do these things consciously, or you'll forget them every time there's a little pressure on you."

Listening to an overly romantic pianist one evening, he said, "The greatest sin in art is not boredom—as everybody says—but lack of proportion and taste. Boredom is only a result." Stabbing the air with a finger, he complained, "Listen to that! Did you ever hear so much *rubato?* And don't look smug; you're almost as bad as he is."

The intricacies of a large work by Bach simply proved beyond me one night, and I admitted my boredom to him. "Harry, as you learn more and more about music, you will come to demand more and more from it intellectually. Bach had the greatest mind of all

composers, and that is why (to all musicians) he is the greatest of
all composers. You will learn; in the meantime, have the decency
to be like everybody else, and *pretend* you enjoy it!"

My adolescent awakening to the artistic world seemed a great
and dramatic thing at the time. Perhaps, truthfully, it was—but I
overplayed my hand. Deciding that I was in truth a Boy Beethoven,
I cranked up for my Suffering Genius act.

One letter home:

"I feel something very strongly. What it is, I don't know exactly,
but it is something which comes only with loneliness. A surging,
powerful drive for—something. A terrible, aching yearning for
something—again, I'm not sure what. I wonder if it was meant
that I be lonely all my life, because it is only with the strength
and drive which come from loneliness that I have ever been able
to accomplish most."

How's that for a letter to the dear family? Dad's reply was almost
as good.

"I notice you report yourself lonely. I have gone to work on
that situation, and I observe that you are seventeen years old and
over five hundred miles away from home for the first time in your
life. This, I must confess, is an extremely deep and devious and
mysterious example of my psychoanalysis and I do not think it
would have occurred to ordinary people."

Seventeen was my year of idealism, of complete confidence in
self, and of my farthest distance from the problem. I thought I
knew more about music then than I think I know about it now. At
seventeen, I knew myself to be a man in everything but years, for
I had all the maturity, attractiveness and understanding of an
adult. There were always elderly ladies or young girls who could
be found to agree with these simple statements of fact.

But I was careful never to mention them near Thaddeus P.
Giddings.

On the horizon of my self-esteem rose only one cloud that I

knew about. Early in the summer came a letter from Dwight
Anderson, of the University of Louisville, who had judged a recent
Kentucky State Piano Contest I had been fortunate enough to win.
He was a true friend, for he wished me well, most cordially, and
tactfully suggested that he was worried about my intellectual integrity. To begin with, he overestimated my intellectual prowess
to think I would know what he was talking about. I honestly did
not understand his meaning at all.

The letter rankled, as truth often does, but I misinterpreted the
reasons why I couldn't get it out of my mind. I reasoned that since
I couldn't dismiss it, and since I was obviously a completely honest
person (I had never *stolen* anything), that it must be a mighty fine
joke. So I went to most of my friends, read it to them, laughed,
and joked, "He sure missed the boat on me, didn't he? Doesn't
know me as well as he thinks he does."

I laughed, and I recall that usually my friends did. I have since
marked them, one by one, as people never to be trusted in an
emergency.

About that time I met a gal, long on both years and experience,
who tried to widen my extramusical horizons a little overmuch.
The nervous wear and tear was rather high, however, and we ended
in a draw. My claims to premature manhood and intellectual integrity fell off noticeably immediately afterwards.

It did not disturb me that musical standards at the National
Music Camp were not stringently professional.

The important thing was that for the first time in my life I
found myself in an environment where music and the arts were
considered a way of life. For the first time I was among people
who did not think it a mark of peculiarity to practice the piano.
For the first time I was hearing good music regularly.

Time after time I discovered that music could thrill me to the
marrow.

On the opening night of camp I played in the flute section as
an orchestra was assembled for an impromptu concert. We began
with Schubert's *Unfinished Symphony*.

Sitting under the arch of an enormous outdoor bowl, awed by
majestic northern pines and a huge lake just behind the amphi-

theater, I fully expected something marvelous to happen. It did. There were no stringed instruments in Paris, Tennessee, and although I had tooted in our high school band, this was my first taste of orchestral playing. Before I knew it the lower strings had begun the first ominous phrase of Schubert's immortal music. Quickly the violins entered with a soul-stirring figure, and they were soon joined by a host of other instruments I had never heard before except on our scratchy phonograph at home. Never before had I suspected the incredible wealth of overtones and color which had been denied me by our tiny record machine. I was filled with the same choking ecstasy of revelation which a colorblind man might feel on suddenly viewing a sunset in all its glory.

One evening the opera class presented scenes from *Faust*. As Marguerite ascended to heaven on a shaft of light, angels could faintly be seen dancing over her on the roof of the outdoor bowl; high above them shone a glittering cross which seemed to be suspended from heaven. Suddenly a marvelous display of northern lights burst forth in the sky above; it seemed as though God Himself had joined hands with the music.

Not all performances of *Faust* turn out so well. There is a famous story about a small opera company in northern England, which performed Faust with rather shabby equipment and scenery. At one point, Mephistopheles was descending to the Underworld through a trap door, when the trap door stuck fast. The audience sat aghast as Mephisto struggled unsuccessfully to climb either in or out of that accursed door. Finally, the horrified silence was cracked by a voice from the gallery which shouted, "Eh, bah goom, lad, 'ell's full up!"

Do not imagine that my Interlochen existence was one of blithe enjoyment alone. Growing up is a beautiful and terrible experience, and my life seemed a hopeless mass of jumbled confusion. In spite of all my foolishness, I was deeply in love—though mercifully for both of us a disparity of ages and religious beliefs made marriage impossible. My musical life was equally frustrating. I suspected that I had talent, but wanted some assurances that I could actually create music, and that I would not just spend the rest of my life condemned to the hopeless gray mediocrity of teaching "It's a Gum Drop Tree" to lazy little girls.

You may recall that I was allowed to go to Interlochen on condition I would enroll at the college in Murray, Kentucky, that fall. My summer's association with music students from all over the country made it seem obvious to me that a small teachers' college was out of the question for anyone except a future "Gum Drop Tree" teacher.

But where to go, and how to justify this about-face to my parents? Thaddeus Giddings, as usual, had an answer.

"Listen to me, ninny." (How I hated to be called that!) "You must not compromise for less than the best. Whenever you're in doubt, go to the top. You'll be surprised: the real top men have always got time to help young boys with the goods."

With that, he marched me off to see Howard Hanson. From camp, it was a long walk to Dr. Hanson's summer home. What would I say to him? Time after time, I tried to organize my thoughts. Twice I got lost and went far out of the way.

There were three other campers at his home when I arrived. He seemed not in the least surprised to see me, but invited me to sit down and continued chatting with the others. What would I say? Here was the director of the great Eastman School of Music, a renowned composer, the first musician I had ever met whose reputation had extended even to the wilds of Paris, Tennessee.

The others left. Dr. Hanson turned to me kindly and asked why I had come. Suddenly it was all blurting out: I didn't know whether to try to be a pianist; I couldn't sight-read; I knew no harmony —had no idea what a dominant seventh was; couldn't play scales; studied forever on one piece, and was seldom ever able to play more than a few pieces at a time. What should I do? Dr. Hanson waited until I had run down before suggesting gently, "Why not try playing for me?" He listened to some Chopin, Beethoven, and a Bach fugue. I turned apprehensively.

"Well, it certainly wasn't as bad as I *expected*," he confided. "I can say that you have talent; how far you will go with it no one can tell. That depends entirely on how hard you are willing to go after what you want."

"But, Dr. Hanson, what about an education? Where should I study?"

"That shouldn't be too hard. I'd be willing to give you a complete scholarship to Eastman"—my heart sang—"but it is too late for this school year. A year from this fall is the earliest we could take you." My heart stopped singing.

"Please, sir—what can I do? Where can I go? I'm so confused I'm going crazy!"

"You're studying with Dorsey Whittington here at Interlochen, are you not? He's a splendid teacher, and the Birmingham Conservatory is close enough to Paris that it shouldn't be too expensive for you to go there. Come on now; it's close to supper and you looked starved—I'll drive you back toward camp."

And so it was done. Dr. Whittington agreed to place me in his class, and I was delighted to understand that it would cost very little more than a year in Murray, Kentucky. This, of course, eliminated any difficulty about getting my parents to consent to the change of plans.

I told my plans to Joey Silverstein, a little thirteen-year-old violinist from Detroit. In spite of his youth, Joey was the most outstanding violinist at camp, and—like me—showed no marked tendency toward malnutrition of the ego. He was unimpressed by the scholarship at Rochester.

"Eastman? What do you want to go there for? Who teaches at Eastman?"

Thaddeus Giddings' voice came back to me: "You must not compromise for less than the best." Where could I go? I had set my heart on Curtis, but their piano class of eighteen selected students was full. As though this scene were preordained, and had been rehearsed ages before, little Joey's voice continued right over my thoughts: "I'm going to Curtis next fall; why don't you try out there? They don't take anything but the best."

It was a long time before I smiled at Joey's unsubtle implication that he was "nothing but the best"; at the time, I was green with envy and would have given my soul for a scholarship to Curtis.

Two days later, I heard someone practicing the Liszt *Hungarian Fantasy for Piano and Orchestra*, a work Russell Baldwin had taught me. It was arresting playing. I had heard every pianist at Interlochen, and knew that not one of them played so lyrically, or with such a warm and effortless vitality. Following the music as a dog follows his nose, I came upon a slim, dark soldier in an abandoned practice hut.

He extended a hand: "I'm Joe Rezits."

During lunch, Joe explained that he was a former camper, back for a sentimental visit before getting out of the army and returning to school. Where? The Curtis Institute of Music, in Philadelphia. My jaw sagged; this was one of those eighteen fabulous piano students—those "nothing-but-the-best" that Joey Silverstein had described!

"Joe, could I get into Curtis?"

"I think you could, but what does that prove? A school like Curtis accepts so few students that sometimes even the most wonderful talents can't get in. You'll just have to try out and see."

"Gosh. They must have some wonderful pianists there."

"The best in the world," he breathed airily. (I was beginning to get the impression that they were not a shy lot of people, either!) "You remember that good-will tour Eugene Ormandy did in Australia? He brought back the best young pianist in the country to study at Curtis. I hear she's really terrific.

"Her name's Nelson—Allison Nelson."

As camp closed, Joe and I went our separate ways.

Neither of us ever dreamed that one day he would be my best friend, and would stand by my side while I married the young girl Eugene Ormandy had brought back from Australia.

Dorsey Whittington satisfied the average man's conception of what a concert pianist ought to be.

Stepping into the Birmingham Conservatory of Music for the first time, I was awe-struck by a huge portrait looming before me: Dorsey the Youth—complete with flowing hair, open collar, sensuous lips and soulful eyes. At the head of the stairs, I feasted mine eyes on a bronze replica of Whittington's head. In one studio I saw a caricature of him. In another I viewed a death mask of Beethoven; close by was a plaster cast of Dorsey's hand.

Trembling with excitement, I was ushered into Whittington's presence. What a change from rustic Interlochen! His was a typical artist's studio. There were two huge pianos, a handsome desk, a portrait of guess-who, tapestries, and the walls were carefully suppressed behind inscribed pictures of virtually every famous musician.

I worshiped at the shrine.

If he had at that moment ordered me to offer myself up as a burnt sacrifice, I should have done so. Instead he told me there had been a slight misunderstanding, and that it would take nearly twice as much money to go to school there as I had understood. If I had had the money, I would have forked it over. As it was, I was merely thunderstruck. With a mental attitude which would hardly have improved my standing at Sunday School, I called Dad from a drugstore downtown. He told me there was no hope for it; I must come back home and go to school in Murray. We simply didn't have the money.

Without supper, I walked up and down the streets of Birmingham until late that night. Finally, exhausted, I sat on a curb in the heart of town and cried my eyes out. I watched all the people going by: beautiful women in fancy cars, college girls with their dates, men hurrying along with briefcases.

I had wild thoughts: Perhaps some rich man will stop and ask what's the matter, and I'll tell him and he'll take out a checkbook and say don't worry and this whole nightmare will be over. . . . But it doesn't happen that way.

I knew one thing. I was not going to give up, and I would not go back to Murray. The next day I marched over Birmingham looking for a job. And the next. By the next day it was apparent that my lack of a trade rendered me useless to everybody. I had studied arc welding in trade school one summer, but could not class as a professional.

Lying awake that night, I tried to make sense out of the mess I was in. What could I do? How about radio? I had done a lot of public speaking and acting; in Interlochen I had done it successfully over the radio. Why not give it a try? "When in doubt, go to the top," echoed Thaddeus Giddings' old voice. The following morning I called on the program director of WBRC, the local NBC radio station, and poured out my whole story.

"Neal," his eyes slipped down to my frayed cuffs, "you might be worth something. I'll give you a call."

I had not yet learned enough about the world to be distrustful of those words, so I waited. The faith of children is a marvelous thing, for three days later he actually *did* call up.

"My number-one news man is quitting next week, and I need someone in a hurry. Come down here."

I came. They handed me several sheets of news and marched out, while an engineer plugged in a microphone and went through the mysterious ritual of his cult. I was plowing through the pages, trying to forewarn myself about any difficult words, when a dreadful thought struck me: how do you read news? I had acted many roles on the radio and stage (badly, by the by), and had done a good bit of that phony elocution known as "oratory," but how do you tell people that a mad dog has bitten a farmer's rump near Suggsville, Alabama? In desperation, I decided to imitate that voice of doom which used to narrate the old *March of Time* films.

A few minutes later John Connolly, the program director, walked back in. "Neal," he looked everywhere but at me, "who on earth taught you to read news?"

All my hopes sank to the ground. I admitted my impromptu imitation of a newsreel announcer.

"I would never have guessed," he mused drily.

Then, "Let me give you a piece of advice. Never imitate anybody or anything—anytime. Next, you've got a good voice, but don't fall in love with it. It may come as a surprise to you to learn that it isn't voice *quality* that makes radio men; it's personality. A man can have the worst voice in creation, but if he's got an interesting vocal personality—he's money.

"I want you to start work at three o'clock tomorrow afternoon."

My radio job didn't allow much time for practicing the piano, but at least it got me through that first year of college. It was work for which I had a natural aptitude, and I enjoyed it immensely. My daily schedule, however, was a killing one. I worked eight hours every night, tried to practice the piano, and insisted on taking a thirty per cent overload in my classroom schedules as well.

Of course I should have cut all other activities to the bone, concentrated on the piano, and tried to get eight hours' good mattress treatment every night. Instead, I studied singing and acting in addition to my other college work, tried to get a job as an actor, and actually did take a job as a church singer on Sundays.

Whittington was a brilliant teacher, but I could not earn enough money to pay my tuition for the Conservatory and practice for the piano lessons at the same time. I was bitter; it seemed obvious that if I meant to become a serious pianist, I would have to go to one of the wealthier schools who could afford to subsidize my studies, leaving my time free for practice.

My voice teacher at the Conservatory, Mrs. Martha McClung, suggested that I take Thaddeus Giddings' advice once again, and "try for the top." "Audition at Curtis," she urged, "and if they don't take you, there's always the scholarship at Eastman open to you." I would have to ask Whittington to prepare me for the Curtis audition, but, fearing an unpleasant scene, I kept putting it off. One day Martha told me that Alexander McCurdy, organ teacher at the Curtis Institute, was to be in Birmingham on one of his concert tours. She shipped me off to play for him. McCurdy was surprisingly accessible, and completely frank.

"I don't know how you can be as ignorant as you are, and play as well as you do. No, I can't tell you whether you can become a concert pianist—you'll just have to audition for Curtis and see what happens."

With Martha's foot on my backside, I finally asked Whittington to prepare me for the audition. His response was not weak.

"Curtis? You don't stand a damn chance!"

After this sociable preliminary, he settled down to work. "All you kids are the same. You want to go to a big-name school in the East. Supposing you graduated from Eastman or Juilliard; where would you be then? They're just degree factories, and don't care anything about you. Once you had that diploma, they'd be through with you.

"But if you'd stay here in Birmingham, you'd be in a school small enough to take a personal interest in you. You can give up this acting and radio foolishness; I'll lend you the money to get through school, and after graduation I'll give you a job till you can pay it off. Nobody else cares about you, but stay here, and I'll push you!"

It was going just the way I had feared. "But, Dr. Whittington, Curtis is a small school, and I wouldn't have to go into debt there."

"Now about Curtis. You haven't got a chance. Certainly you have talent, but you're seventeen years old. They only want child prodigies.

"Besides, who teaches at Curtis? Don't let Serkin's name fool you; Vengerova's the real teacher at Curtis and I daresay you don't know anything about her or her theories. Serkin's away on tour most of the year, and is hardly ever in school. You stay here; you'll have me for piano, and I've got one of the best theory men in the country downstairs. That's the backbone of your musical education. All you need to do is settle down to practicing eight hours a day. That's the real secret of advancement, you know. A teacher can't *hand* you much knowledge, but he can help you to find it for yourself.

"What's the difference between a $50 teacher and a $15 teacher? Not too much, sometimes. But when you pay $50 for a music lesson you go home and work like a dog trying to get your money's worth. No wonder you improve faster than you do for a man you're not afraid of."

There was a compelling intelligence behind Whittington's remarks, but the conversation seemed completely out of control from my point of view. Dr. Whittington was becoming impassioned, and I seemed farther away from Curtis than ever. "Maybe I might get in on a fluke," I ventured.

"All right. For the argument, suppose you did get in. Let's see . . ." he made mental calculations. "Curtis," he stood up, "has graduated perhaps four pianists a year for the last twenty-five years; that makes a hundred piano graduates, all of whom were capable of playing first-class concerts. The catch is," and he made his point triumphantly, "there aren't a hundred concert pianists in the country today who make their living from that source alone. And only a handful of *those* come from Curtis."

His voice softened at my distress. "The obvious trouble is that there just isn't much room at the top.

"Just think of all those pianists who got out of school thinking they were going to set the world on fire. Some of them did play concerts, and found out it wasn't such a hot life after all—but you young people never believe that. Nearly all of them suffered a thousand frustrations, and finally had to go back to teaching out in the woods somewhere to make a living.

"Harry—" he was obviously in earnest—"give yourself a break.

"Save yourself all those sleepless nights, all the agonizing self-doubts, the heartaches, the disappointments. Give up now, before you've torn yourself to pieces over this thing. There's a good life for you here if you'll just stop fighting the air, and make your place where you find it.

"There are plenty of ways to serve music without playing concerts.

"One last word. Those eastern schools all know me, and any of them will take you or reject you on my say-so. If you insist, I'll have to give the necessary permission for your audition at Curtis, but I will not recommend you to them."

That night I was initiated to some of those self-doubts he had mentioned.

David Gibson, my roommate, was a brilliant pianist, and had considered auditioning with me. After I described Whittington's arguments to him, he declined to make the trip.

What should I do?

I had expected Whittington's arguments all to run his own way, but hadn't expected them to scare me so. He was obviously speaking sincerely about the impossibility of a concert career. Could I make the grade? Was I just going up to Philadelphia to make a fool out of myself? To waste my transportation money, and arouse my teacher's ire besides? What chance would I have when my own teacher refused to recommend me?

Why not do as he said? Give up now. Make my place where I found it. How comfortable it would be to relax and accept his guidance.

No. I did not want to teach. I loved music too much to torture my ears struggling with wretched pupils who could not be made to practice. It would be far better to earn a living in radio or acting, and enjoy music as a rewarding hobby.

But more doubts: Thaddeus Giddings had claimed there was always room at the top. Whittington said there was no room, and had figures to back it up. What was I to think?

If only I would do what he said, and conform to the pattern, I could make a nice place for myself down here. And it *would* be such a comfortable answer for all my problems.

At that moment I made a chance discovery which justified every minute I had ever spent studying drama. Just while imagining that it would be "comfortable" to do as Whittington said, I flipped open a book of Sophocles' plays I had been studying. For several pages I tried, fruitlessly, to concentrate, as my troubled thoughts returned again and again to Whittington and his advice. Suddenly my spine crawled—but what was it? I read the passage again. And again and again. Down twenty-four hundred years, Sophocles' voice spoke to me through Electra's withering retort:

"Cowards believe such comfortable things."

I would *not* give in. I *would* go to Philadelphia. And I would not settle for less than what I wanted. I would play concerts or give up music as a career.

Several weeks later I stood and stared at the Curtis Institute of Music. Almost a quarter of a century before it had been converted from one of Philadelphia's fine mansions. Situated at the edge of a little park known as Rittenhouse Square, the handsome gray building still radiated a feeling of calm elegance.

I had already been inside the school for a practice session before my audition, and had been awed by the music which came from its studios, the beautiful carpeting, the fine paintings, and above all the profusion of splendid pianos. Before this time most of my practice had been done on whatever dilapidated uprights were available, the few "good" pianos I had known usually having been reserved for great occasions. Here, every studio seemed to have a first-class professional instrument.

Now, in a brief rest before my audition, I surveyed the school from across the street. Very soon now I would have ten minutes in which to start being a concert pianist, or start being something else. Ten minutes was such a long, short time. What if I got stage-fright and broke down? Was it fair to base my whole life on only ten minutes' playing?

Yes, it was. Every man must draw a line sometime, and this was mine.

They required me to bring a Beethoven sonata, a Bach prelude and fugue, and two works by Chopin—one brilliant, one slow. Which would they ask for? I had pinned my hopes on a Chopin nocturne; in view of my poor technique, they would have to consider me on musicality alone. Surely the "slow" Chopin was required for just that reason.

Two black-haired boys wandered out of school and in my direction. Glancing at my telltale brief case, one asked, "Auditioning?"

"Yes, sir."

"Scared?"

"Yes, sir."

He smiled. "You don't have to 'sir' me. My name is Sherman Frank. This is Ted Lettvin. We study with Serkin."

"Can they really tell? In ten minutes, I mean?"

"Sure; they know in thirty seconds—the rest is just courtesy."

My face must have betrayed the lump in my throat. While Ted wandered off on an errand, Sherman turned to me. "Relax. Stop worrying—what's your name?—Harry. They're the best in the world in there, and they know what they're listening for. You could make all the mistakes in the world just because you were scared, and they would know why you made them. No matter how badly you play, they'll be able to hear what they're listening for. So relax."

Beethoven's *Appassionata* thundered across the street to us from the huge corner studio in which auditions are held. It was a work totally beyond me at the time, both technically and musically. "I don't stand a chance," I muttered. "I don't know what I'm doing here."

"That's crazy talk, boy. What Beethoven are you playing?"

"*Opus 7 in E-flat.*"

"Well, that's a change. They've been listening to the *Appassionata* and *Waldstein* all morning."

Whittington had suggested the sonata for that very reason: apparently he knew what he was talking about. With a wave of remorse, I admitted that he must also be right about my inability to compete with pianists such as the one Sherman and I were hearing now. I broke out, "Every pianist this morning has played better than I do! I was a *fool* to come!"

A number of noisy students headed across the street, and Sherman pulled me to a secluded corner. "Listen, kid, I'll tell you some-

thing I don't tell everybody. When I took my audition here, I felt
the same way. I listened to all those other kids, and they played
rings around me. It was so hopeless that I went home and cried all
afternoon. But they took me.

"You've got to understand it takes something more than fingers
to be a pianist. They can *give* you the fingers, if you've got the
rest. If you're as bad as you say you are, it means you got to this
audition on raw talent alone: without even hearing you, I'm going
to bet you make it."

I did not follow that last bit of reasoning.

My audition was a nightmare.

Heart thumping, I walked in and promptly broke one of the most
sacred Curtis canons. It was a hot day in May, and I had never
owned enough coats to be comfortable wearing one while playing.
Not only that, but I had never before been in an atmosphere where
shirt sleeves were taboo.

"May I take off my coat?"

Instead of a simple "yes," there was a sudden conference at the
other end of the room. Horrified at the consequences of my question, I stared at the auditioning board. Mr. Serkin and Mr. Zimbalist
I recognized from their pictures. Also present were a heavy, dark-
haired woman, and a tiny, gray-haired man. To one side sat a
slender, elderly lady, peacefully knitting away and watching the
show.

I was amazed that coat-removal proved such an issue, and too
frightened to retract my request. Finally, permission was granted
by unanimous consent, and I sat down. Would I play the Bach,
please? The prelude went well, but a black sea overwhelmed my
mind in the fugue. Disaster. (Oh, *why* did I ever come here?) I
saved the day by turning to make one of those penetrating observations which have so marked my career.

"I forgot."

Everyone giggled, I got permission to try again, and bungled
through without further disaster. I should never have come, I
thought; it's all finished, now. I very nearly quit trying. They asked
for snatches of each of the remaining works, and disappointed me
by stopping the Chopin nocturne before I got to the juicy place

where I felt I was *so* romantic. Why are they torturing me by dragging this out, now that I've ruined everything? Why don't they let me go? Suddenly, it was over.

Walking to the door, I felt frustrated. I had played badly, and settled nothing. On an impulse, I turned.

"May I ask an opinion?"

Flutter. They had been reading my letters of recommendation. Somebody looked at somebody else. What did he say? He wants an opinion. Somebody looks back at me. Just what do I want to know?

I was in over my head. There was nothing for it but to keep going. "I want to know whether I have enough talent to be a concert pianist. I mean, regardless of whether you take me or not. I want to be a pianist, but if there are any limits on how good I can be, I don't want to fool with it. I can make my living other ways, and I'd rather do that than teach." (I forgot that all these people were teachers!)

More flutter. Heads together. Somebody reads from what is obviously Whittington's permission-but-not-recommendation letter. Finally: "Would you come back about 5:00 this afternoon when the auditions are over?"

The school registrar told me how to get to a restaurant, but I was too excited to go in and eat. Instead, I walked until three-thirty in the afternoon, and then presented myself back at Curtis so as not to be late for my five-o'clock appointment. I needn't have hurried; the auditions ran a half hour late.

For two hours I sat. Soon Joe Rezits came by, and we perched on the steps chattering about my audition. Sylvia Zaremba sat with us for a time, and Joe introduced me to Jacob Lateiner and Seymour Lipkin as they wandered by. I had never heard of them, but took his word that they were outstanding students. Joe identified the strangers at my audition as Mme. Vengerova (his teacher) and Mr. Horszowski. The motherly knitter was Mrs. Zimbalist, who had founded the school. Second by second I reconstructed the audition for him; he was delighted that I'd taken off my coat, he consoled my memory failure, and together we speculated on the significance of my appointment that afternoon.

"Perhaps," he marveled, "they'll accept you on the spot!"

I went in to my second appointment so tense that I shivered as

if in a chill. Mme. Vengerova spoke for the board, and put questions
to me about my repertoire, my length of study, my school grades,
what I would do if I gave up music, and how I practiced. On this
point I ventured to elaborate and explained that I had never practiced enough.

Mme. Vengerova cut me off quietly wtih a smile. "Yes, we know;
you have many bad habits." I had never spoken with foreigners
before, and was fascinated by the slow, measured accent with
which she spoke. Her heavy, Russian voice continued quietly, "It is
very difficult to say how far one may go in music. There are so
many things to consider."

I was still waiting for a simple yes or no answer to my questions.
Instead, she smiled enigmatically and thanked me for coming. Her
last words were, "You will hear from us."

Did this mean they had not the heart to say "no" to my face? I
boarded my train in a state of great agitation, for I suspected the
worst.

The following Monday morning I was eighteen years old, and
celebrated by going back to school in Birmingham. My dear voice
teacher, Martha McClung, believed in miracles. "Wouldn't it be a
lovely birthday present if you were to hear from them today?"

But there was little chance. Someone had told me that it might
be another two or three weeks before I was notified of Curtis'
decision.

Returning to my boardinghouse just before lunch, I shoved a
routine hand into the mailbox; it came out clutching a long white
envelope from the Curtis Institute of Music. For perhaps a half
hour I sat on the front porch swing, looking at that envelope.
Dazedly, I noticed that there was no period after "Mr" in the
address. Someone knocked on the door of Virgil Trucks' (the Detroit
Tigers' pitcher) house across the street. I remembered the first "we-
regret-to-inform-you" letter I had gotten from Curtis after applying
for an audition the year before. What would this one say? Here, in
this envelope, was the rest of my life.

At long last, I pried the flap loose, taking infinite pains to break
only the glue seal, and not to tear any shred of that sacred paper.
But I still could not take the single sheet out of the envelope.

Finally, "I'll take it out just as if it were only a letter!" Quickly, the paper flipped out and open:

> "The Director asks me to inform you
> that you have been accepted . . ."

My eyes could see no farther. "You have been accepted . . ."
Accepted.
Accepted!
I started walking sedately toward school. Within fifty feet I was running madly, laughing, shouting wild greetings to every person I saw. I roared through the back door of the Conservatory and plunged into Martha's studio: "I made it! I'm in! *They took me!*"

With a shriek, she flung her arms about me, and we laughed, and kissed, and danced around the room, and yelled just to hear the noise. After exhausting ourselves, we fell into a couple of chairs, still laughing insanely. Finally, we calmed down. One glance at each other, and we were howling again. We continued this way: unable to look each other in the eye without bursting out anew in another fit of laughter.

At last, an idea struck Martha. She choked off a laugh, and asked, "Have you told Dorsey?"

In such moments, murders are planned.

Years later, I came to love Dorsey Whittington as a true friend, and to see that there had always been two sides to the controversies between us. After growing a little myself, it was easy to see that his bravura exterior had hidden from me one crucial fact: he was just as good as he said he was.

At the time, however, I hated the man. Telling him of my acceptance at Curtis gave me more good clean fun than I could have had by any means short of killing him outright.

"Dr. Whittington, I heard from Curtis."

"Yes? What did they say?"

"They took me."

"Well, I'll be damned. The school must be going downhill."

ISABELLE VENGEROVA

Dr. Freud says our minds avoid the unpleasant. Certainly it is with great reluctance and difficulty that I force my mind back through those terrible years at Curtis.

I arrived in Philadelphia full of ignorance, hopes and confusion. Almost instantly I was thrown into the tiger-pit of professional artistic standards. I gained some idea of what good piano playing was, even though I did not do much of it myself. But the experience proved such a ruthless and searing one—indeed, it could hardly have been anything else—that I suffered a complete moral breakdown. It was years before I could bring myself even to speak of my days at Curtis without a most exquisite anguish; I would go to any lengths of lying or subterfuge to avoid the subject altogether.

Present-day piano teaching is the result of a specialized evolution which has taken place mostly in the last three hundred years.

Domenico Scarlatti (1685-1757) is considered to have founded the modern concept of virtuoso piano playing. He was an astonishing technician for his day, and after him came more and better ones, but none seemed able to meet the challenge laid down by Niccolo Paganini (1782-1840), whose technical skill convinced his contemporaries that his soul had been sold to the devil in return for an unholy wizardry on the violin. Finally, in the nineteenth century, Franz Liszt (1811-1886) burst forth on the musical scene with a pianistic splendor which many say has never been equaled.

The mechanics of piano playing up to and including Liszt seem strangely faulty by present standards. Liszt, in spite of his greatness, seems to have played with a rigid, tense arm. The greatest woman pianist of the day (Clara Schumann, wife of the composer) suffered from the same fault. Liszt's intimates report the results of this tenseness by relating that in later years he was concerned that

73

some of his technique seemed to be slipping away, somewhat as a singer might lose her vocal prowess after forcing her voice too long.

The stage thus set, Theodor Leschetizky made his entrance, with an approach to teaching which completely revolutionized piano playing. His idea was as revolutionary as Dr. Read's present-day theory of natural childbirth, and quite similar to it in principle. He believed that most of the harmful effects from physical effort are caused when a necessary working muscle finds itself confronted and frustrated by another muscle pulling in opposition to it. In other words, if you tense your entire arm or body, the muscles you need to use have to overcome the resistance of all the other needlessly tensed muscles before they can accomplish the task at hand, whether it is striking a piano keyboard or giving birth to a child. Leschetizky founded the great "relaxation" school of piano playing, which forms the basis of almost every pianist's technique today.

To name his pupils is to recite the catalog of pianists and teachers who are responsible for today's pianistic generation. Paderewski, the greatest pianist of his day, was a pupil of Leschetizky. The late Artur Schnabel, perhaps the world's leading authority on Beethoven, studied with him. Brailowsky, considered by many to be our great Chopin exponent, was a Leschetizky product. Edwin Hughes and Horszowski were pupils of his.

Perhaps the greatest pedagogue produced by Theodor Leschetizky was Isabelle Vengerova, a young girl from Minsk, Russia, who came to study with him in Vienna late in the nineteenth century. Vengerova continued her studies with Mme. Essipoff (one of Leschetizky's assistants, and the second of his various wives) and later taught at the Imperial Conservatory in St. Petersburg.

She became to the piano what Leopold Auer was to the violin. You could not become a violinist in Holy Russia without studying with Auer, it was said. One only need consider that Auer produced Heifitz, Elman and Zimbalist, among others, to see the reason why.

Mme. Vengerova came to be considered by many as the greatest living piano teacher. She had a conception of piano playing which was uniquely her own. Technique and musicianship were inseparable. Uncannily, she dissected the anatomy of musical intuition, and reduced it to terms understandable by every student. She established an artistic conscience in her pupils, and knew how to make them delve deeper and deeper within themselves in an unending search for perfection. And she got results. A few of her pupils are Leonard Bernstein, Lukas Foss, Samuel Barber, Thomas Scherman, Zadel Skolovsky, Leonard Pennario, Sol Kaplan, Sylvia Zaremba, Gary Graffman, Jacob Lateiner, Jean Graham, Lillian Kalir, and her own nephew, Nicholas Slonimsky.

Dorsey Whittington had asked, "What makes a great pedagogue?"

Almost any $3.00-an-hour teacher can outline the basic principles of good piano playing just the same as a $50.00 teacher. The difference is that the great teacher understands that each of these principles is a matter of life and death, rather than just a friendly bit of advice on a rainy Saturday morning. It is one thing to say, "Play the right notes," and another to eradicate the possibility of wrong ones. It is one thing to say, "Obey the composer's markings," and quite another to respect them so intensely that any tiniest infraction is a matter for immediate violent countermeasures.

Each of us has within him the seeds of greatness, and all of us have known the feeling that we possessed potentialities beyond anything we ever realized. The great problem for the teacher is how to cause the ignorant, the lazy and the undisciplined to dig deep enough within their own potentialities to realize that genius which is the essence of man.

Vengerova was hardly a believer in progressive education. Her word was law, and to fall short of her expectations was to welcome disaster. She was a tyrannical disciplinarian. For someone accustomed to America's let-the-little-darlings-express-themselves educational methods, entering her studio could be like waking up in a Spanish Inquisition.

Her great weapon was fear.

And fear works: The records are full of people who have performed "impossible" feats while motivated by great fear. Frail women have exhibited great strength while saving their children from burning buildings, and men have been known to lift huge weights while saving loved ones from terrible accidents.

Vengerova had that gift for human psychology which is one of the most underestimated attributes of the Russian people. There are those who say the Soviet system must fail because its people are afraid. And yet I can testify to a fear which was inseparable from worshipful devotion, to the conviction that there could be no faults except my own, to a rigid discipline which seemed more an honor than a burden. In the lowest depths of my despair with Vengerova I was offered an opportunity to study with another great teacher. My reply was one of absolute allegiance: I would not leave her; if she could not make a pianist of me, it could not be done.

Perhaps I was right. In order to shake me out of my hopelessly amateurish approach to music, a complete personal and pianistic rebirth was necessary. Such rebirths are not always happy experiences. I can at least testify that I would certainly not be a pianist today, had it not been for Isabelle Vengerova.

On the debit side, her forceful personality aroused my naturally rebellious nature. Also, I had some finger problems which she may not have diagnosed correctly; perhaps another teacher would have been better for them. This situation sprang from an over-refinement of the original Leschetizky "method." Leschetizky, by the way, claimed that he had no "method"—that he just went after musical results and adapted his approach to the needs of each pupil.

Leschetizky avoided percussive playing (raising the finger before striking the key) *in performance*. He was, however, clearly on record as favoring practicing with raised fingers (percussively, in other words) in order to develop strength and finger independence. Perhaps he fell prey to one of the dangers of founding a "system," or "method": that the disciples of that method usually tend to become more dogmatic about side issues than the original creator was.

This may all seem a minor point to the layman, but it is an important matter and a source of much confusion and contention among pianists. Critics of the Leschetizky method quote him as having said the fingers "should be like relaxed bands of steel." "How," they ask, "can fingers ever get the strength of steel if they are *relaxed* all the time?" The answer is that Leschetizky advocated slow practice with raised fingers to develop strength and independence. There are photographs of Leschetizky demonstrating his ideas of practice, and in which his own fingers are reared up like stallions.

The reason to avoid percussive playing in actual performance is that it is more tiring physically, and produces a harsher, more brittle sound than notes which are depressed by a finger already in position and touching the key. As a source of tonal variety, many artists desire this change in sound quality, and like to play percussively sometimes in order to get a brilliant effect in certain kinds of passage work. There is good evidence that even Vengerova raised her fingers in her earlier years.

By the time I reached Mme. Vengerova, however, her thinking had developed to the point that it was an unforgivable sin if one's finger so much as flickered above a key in either practice or performance. Considering that one of my gravest problems was that of weak and unco-ordinated fingers, it seems understandable that my hands were in some ways strangely slow to develop under her tutelage.

And yet those who study piano with a teacher are not studying pedagogy. They do not have the whole picture. Some things they will do naturally, and the teacher may leave them unmentioned for fear of arousing the pupil's conceit. All the lesson time is devoted to the pupil's ills, and not to his good points; it is a mistake for him then to go forth relating his experiences as an account of the master's "method." He has actually seen only one facet of the system he proposes to describe.

I shall simply tell you what happened to me.

Machiavelli advised that if a prince had to choose between love and fear, he should determine to be feared.

Fear alone, however, would hardly have served Vengerova's purpose. It might have produced a large external effort, but would not have induced me to undertake the self-searching inner revolution she was seeking to bring about.

Love alone would have lost her my respect, and would not have given the necessary sense of desperate urgency to my efforts. I had been a "teacher's pet" many times; looking back, I must admit that I often ingratiated myself (how we hate to admit these things, even to ourselves!) and frequently used it as a device to escape doing any more work than was absolutely necessary. There were sometimes touching personal relationships, but they added little to my pianistic growth.

Vengerova needed both emotions. It was unlikely that love could be added to fear, but quite possible indeed to add fear to love. So we had a honeymoon. I became the most favored of students. Madame

came down from New York for a day and a half each week to teach
the eight pupils who studied with her at the Curtis Institute. I was
commissioned to meet that train each week, and her other students
turned green with envy. Joe Rezits, whom I'd met at Interlochen,
announced it was a signal honor when my lesson time was placed
immediately before lunch. I didn't understand.

"Haven't they told you?" he asked. "There are no morning classes
at Curtis because everyone is expected to practice on his instrument
during the first part of the day, when his mind is freshest. If your
lesson was first thing in the morning, there wouldn't be time to
practice before it. If it was right after lunch, you'd be too nervous
to eat. Any time after that, you'd have to leave class and go in to
your lesson 'cold.' The way it is, you can practice all morning, go
to your lesson, eat lunch (if it was a good lesson), and then go to
class." I marveled at how I had managed things.

Curtis places a Steinway grand piano in the room of each piano
major, thus ending the practice problems found at most other
schools. I inherited the instrument formerly used by Eugene
Istomin, who had just left school. "A good sign," whispered Joe,
though this may have been undue optimism.

On the way to my first lesson, he had made my head swirl with
last-minute advice, like a desperate parent sending his child off to
its first party. "If she asks you why you want to study with her, say
you heard some of her pupils play and that you liked their tone and
musicianship. Don't say anything about technique; just 'tone and
musicianship.' That always makes a good impression on her. And
when you play for her, just be sure it's *very* romantic. She knows
you have no technique, but warm playing will remind her how
musical you are.

"And don't make her repeat anything . . . try to memorize everything she says . . . she may ask you at any time to repeat whatever
she just said, because she feels that you don't really understand a
thing unless you can tell it to someone else. If your mind wanders,
and you can't repeat what she said—look out!

"Don't make her mad," was his parting shot. "Don't ever disagree
with her!"

Once in the studio, I could not understand Joe's concern about
Vengerova's temper. Madame seemed like a majestic grandmother.

She was not tall, but marvelously imposing. Age and overweight
made her movements away from the piano rather slow and stately.
Her dress was cut somewhat along the lines of a gunny sack.
Around her, I always wanted to speak in a hushed voice, the way
one does in a church on Tuesdays.

To my relief, no questions came about "why I wanted to study
with her."

I had prepared a few pieces, and she listened to them politely.
Afterwards there were many questions about my background,
musical and personal. My ignorance seemed abysmal. Whom had
my teachers studied with? I hardly knew; one, I said, had worked
with a pupil of Leschetizky. A look of annoyance flitted across her
face as she informed me that I must be mistaken. I knew I was
right and started to say so.

"Oh, but . . ." (Joe's voice whispered in my ear, "Don't ever disagree with her!") ". . . perhaps she didn't," I finished lamely. Unwilling to seem a complete fool, I fought back to give a good account of myself. The question came, "How do you practice?" I
tried to give a particularly clear answer.

"I work on every new piece quite slowly, and then repeat it over
and over until . . . until it goes."

"And when a difficulty presents itself in the music . . . how do
you untie such a Gordian knot?"

I divined that she wanted to know what I did about a hard place.
Still fighting, I reached back for every rule of practice I had ever
heard (and seldom obeyed). "First I take each hand separately, and
then put them together slowly and go over it some more . . . until
it goes," I finished as before. Why, I wanted to know, was she
smiling?

"You are like a child," came her measured, gravelly, almost hyp-
notic voice, "drawing innocent pictures in the sand." She drew a deep
breath. "And now, my boy," her voice had changed briskly, "let us
begin." I thought we had been having a lesson for the last twenty
minutes, but now I learned my error.

She began at the beginning.

"How you sit at the piano." Madame directed my body. "Sit
erect; straighten your back . . . no, not stiff. Sit like a good horseman on his horse, and yield to the movements of your arms as far

as necessary, much as the horseman might yield to the movements of his steed. . . . You are from the South. Do you know horses?"

"Oh, no," I replied. Somewhere in the filing rooms of her incredible mind a drawer snapped shut, and horses were never again used as a comparison in my lessons.

"Now, your arms . . . do not flap your elbows when you play. You look like a goose trying to take flight. Try to hold them still and relaxed . . . so. Of course it has nothing to do with the music, but this is not graceful, what you do. Chopin said that if your playing looked well it probably sounded well . . . you like Chopin?" My head pumped up and down; another drawer snapped open in her mind: Chopin could be used again. "Many pianists feel that nothing matters except the actual sounds they produce. This is not quite true. The listener's ear should first be seduced through the eye, and thus be rendered more impressionable."

After placing my body before the keyboard, she explained a system of playing in which all muscles were relaxed except those absolutely essential to depressing each key. Even those muscles were to be relaxed immediately after striking the key, for then the hand's weight alone was sufficient to keep the key lowered. If this sudden relaxation were complete, it would be accompanied by a dipping of the wrist, for there should be no muscles tense enough even to hold up the forearm. Such an attack, she explained, produced the most beautiful known piano sound. Moreover, it was a technique which, once acquired, was never lost. Her pupils required only a week or two of practice in order to get their hands back, or regain their technique, even after years in the army. Training the muscles to relax after every effort, like the action of one's heart, had the added advantage of giving a pianist almost limitless endurance.

We practiced this motion again and again.

I was amazed at the amount of work required to play only one note. Slow practice I had heard of before, but here there would be as much as two minutes of hard concentrated relaxation between each note. Just to play one note there seemed so many things to keep track of; I was successful at first, but then began to lose control of details. A finger arched slightly, and poised in the air before striking its key.

"*Verboten,*" her voice crackled.

Moments later my elbow waggled, and moments later my right forearm failed to relax enough.

"You must try to extend your span of concentration, Harry."

Immediately, she leaned back from the piano and relaxed me by telling droll stories, each with some little moral for me. I giggled heartily at comparisons of my playing to children she had known in Russia, running along boardwalks at the beach. The boards, like my wrists, would dip slightly when the bare young feet landed on them, and then the children would leap high in the air to avoid contact with the hot planks as long as possible.

"To learn real relaxation, Harry, you should watch the movements of a cat. Have you ever owned a cat? Do you like them?"

Two more negative replies from me, and cats followed horses to the limbo of things not to use on Harry Neal. This, in spite of the fact that Madame loved cats and often used them to illustrate her points with other pupils. She was still feeling about for subjects which would excite my quick enthusiasm.

We resumed our exercises, and suddenly the hour was over. She assigned the Chopin *C-sharp minor Étude* for the following week. Just as I gathered my books, she gave me a quizzical look:

"It was not so terrible after all, was it?"

My confusion over this question was covered when she granted me the indescribable honor of walking down the stairs beside her. Chatting and basking in reflected glory whenever she was stopped by admiring well-wishers, I ceremoniously opened the massive front door of the Institute and accompanied her across the street to the Warwick Hotel, where she was to have lunch.

My joy knew no bounds.

For the next few weeks I seemed incapable of any wrong. Rumors of her ferocious temper filtered down to me, but I seemed to lead a charmed life. Student tales would circulate now and then about her throwing a small statue at Jacob Lateiner in a fit of passion, about growing so angry with Abba Bogin that her nose began to bleed, and about her tearing Harriet Shirvan's music in half, stamping on it and pointing at the door.

But on me she always smiled. When my span of concentration showed some minor improvement, she was quick to applaud. If I missed a little practice now and then, she seemed not to notice.

Never before, though, had I been exposed to such absolute concentration. "The way to make a true *legato* is thus," she said. "Do not raise the first finger until the second has struck its note. For *legatissimo* you hold the first note yet a little longer."

In spite of all rumors, she never gave a hint of exasperation, but let one finger raise a fraction of a moment too soon or too late for a true *legato,* even in some hidden inner voice, and there was an instant correction. Let a thirty-second note be blurred ever so slightly, and there was an instant correction. Perhaps most difficult and important of all, let there be the faintest unwanted variation in tone quality, and there was an instant correction. The acuteness of her ear and her relentless concentration were legendary.

She asked if I was sure about my tempo in the Chopin étude. The metronome marking showed eighty-eight beats per minute. There was no metronome in the room, so I glanced at my watch and tapped out three beats every two seconds.

"Well," she beamed. "How clever. What a resourceful young man you are."

It is a tribute to the conceit of the human animal that I considered myself to be quite worthy of these extravagances on her part. The more she singled me out, the more my little ego was flattered, and the more I was reduced to a worshipful lap-dog who would have gladly died to satisfy a whim of hers. Though I did sometimes fail to practice.

Yes, I ate it up. When she asked questions I babbled cheerily away, confident that nothing I did would ever be too very wrong. All the while she fed me little bits of rope, and watched. And tested. And waited. I completely misread the signs and happily assumed that things would always remain as they then were.

I was like a little lamb, thoughtlessly kicking its heels after entering the slaughtering pen.

The day came when Vengerova asked no further questions. She had made up her mind; I was to be wrenched from one way of life, and forcibly implanted in another one. Midway through my sixth lesson I played a little Schumann novelette for her.

"That was quite good," she said. "But in a year you will regard it as child's play. In a year you will be doing things you now consider impossible. But this was quite good. Yes, by the standards you have always known, it was very good work.

"And that, my boy," she continued pleasantly but firmly, "is the last easy compliment you will ever get in this studio." Her heavy Russian voice went on:
"You have now entered another world."

From almost the first day of school, Joe Rezits was my closest friend.

At my first lesson, Mme. Vengerova had suggested that another of her students, Jacob Lateiner, supervise my work during the week. Like me, Jacob was inclined to be lazy; unlike me, he was a fine pianist. After working hard on my Chopin étude, I carried it to him memorized and at the correct tempo, though correct in little else. He tried to be encouraging.

"Well, at least you can memorize."

We talked for the rest of the evening, and he told me all about Rembrandt and anti-Semitism. We became good friends but somehow never did many finger exercises.

The next week or so, Madame asked Joe to look after me, and what a well-suited pair we were! Joe and I needed one another. He needed someone to look down on, and I needed someone to lean on. The halt led the blind, and together we shuffled along.

Night after night he pumped me full of lore. I learned the "Curtis whistle," which was three shorts and a long: the first four notes of Beethoven's *Fifth Symphony,* also known as the "V for Victory" of World War II. How grandly esoteric I felt each evening to whistle those notes outside his nearby rooming-house window, and catch the key he soon tossed down! How amusing and penetrating and bilingual I thought myself when repeating the Jewish jokes and proverbs he taught me!

I learned that when one Vengerova student asked another how he was getting along, the immediate rejoinder should be, "I'm having my ups and downs," in reference to her characteristic wrist motion. We could then all laugh at our own cleverness. I learned that all Mr. Serkin's students had big techniques, but were to be regarded as playing like cobblers, and that their musicianship wasn't worth a damn. In the interests of human charity, however, we would treat them tolerantly.

A Vengerova student majoring in composition got together with Joe and wrote a little waltz with variations in the style of Brahms.

They recorded it while a metronome, set at about seventy-eight beats per minute, clicked away beside the microphone. Getting back to school after a summer's vacation, they proclaimed the discovery of an unknown Brahms work, actually recorded by Brahms. They had re-recorded this priceless find, and here it was! The metronome clicks were explained as a crack in the original record, and this detail removed all doubts.

They were a sensation. A throng (twelve people made a "throng" at Curtis) gathered to hear the great discovery. Seymour Lipkin, a Serkin student and therefore open to no mercy whatsoever, put his hand to his head and proclaimed, "Now we shall all take a lesson from the great master himself!" After making fools out of everyone, the boys announced their hoax. This second sensation was as good as the first. Seymour's girl, an Australian named Allison Nelson, found the deception decidedly unfunny. However, she was a Serkin student also, and her sense of humor therefore suspect.

It was not long before Joe had introduced me to everyone at Curtis; there were only about a hundred and fifty students in all. Sherman Frank, who had given such excellent advice at my audition, was still there, and so was his friend Teddy Lettvin. I enjoyed comparing students at the school. If a passage was written for one hand alone, the Serkin pupils invariably played it that way, while Mme. Vengerova unhesitatingly split it up between the hands if she thought it would improve the playing. I thought her approach far more sensible.

On the other hand, Mme. Vengerova worked from "edited" music. That is, music which some authority had filled in with phrase and dynamic markings, pedalings, etc. The problem with such editions is that often you cannot tell which are the composer's markings and which the editor's. Serkin students returned to the fountainhead and worked from original scores which had only the composer's own markings in them. I was inclined to feel they were right in doing so.

Mostly, however, Joe and I talked about Vengerova and girls. There was an urgency in our late-night discussions of Vengerova which was matched only by the fervor of our late-night discussions of girls.

My late nights were causing me to get up later in the mornings, and therefore to practice less. Vengerova seemed not to notice, and

I assumed that this must be because magic just naturally flowed from my fingers.

Even after her announcement that the honeymoon was over, I remained unworried. Later in that lesson, I had gotten still another pleasant compliment. The following week I suffered a memory lapse in the Bach *D minor Prelude and Fugue,* and she grunted, "Good . . . Good!" when I was able to pick up the threads and continue playing without a break in the rhythm. My position seemed so secure that I felt quite free in exploring my new life.

About this time a friend outside of school asked if I would accommodate him by escorting his girl friend's sister to a concert. He had a "heavy" date in prospect and didn't want Sister around. He would even pay for the tickets.

This gal was not what Joe and I had envisioned as the maiden most likely to Deepen and Ennoble my Art. She was shortish, a little plump, and her looks were what might be described damningly as "all right." On the other hand, she had a nice smile and could be sent into a passion by serious music. As an added advantage, I didn't have to get up the nerve to ask her for a date, this being done for me. We dated some more, and I began to believe my friend was working on the wrong sister. She and I had dates until quite late at night several times that week and my practice suffered badly.

Ignoring Joe's advice to get a good night's sleep before every lesson, I even stayed out with her until the wee hours on the night before my eighth lesson with Mme. Vengerova. Those charitably inclined might say my foolishness was "normal," but it was also very wrong. I was in Philadelphia to do a job, and that job was to make a supreme effort at every moment. Wasting my time amounted to a betrayal of trust.

For me, the wrath of Isabelle Vengerova was only hours away.

The time had now come for fear.

I once asked Vengerova why my left hand, which had always been considered backward in its development, seemed to progress so much more rapidly (under her training) than my right. She replied, "It is because your left hand was so underdeveloped that it did not have any bad habits for me to overcome."

The whole of Harry Neal was a mass of bad habits. In order to build a new structure which could stand any storm, it would be necessary to destroy the old one. She now set about to destroy the Harry Neal who had been.

Some of her unhappy pupils like to dismiss Vengerova as a cruel and often sadistic woman. In the interests of accuracy, I shall not try to tell you what went on inside her mind. Perhaps, sometimes, she may have enjoyed twisting the knife. But I have known pupils of hers to leave, infuriated, after a few lessons (or even only one interview), because of the terrible self-doubts she raised in them. Years later they could be found still quoting from memory almost every word she had spoken to them, and often still practicing hard to prove she was wrong. Beloved or not, she was a vastly constructive force in their lives. Whether she had this effect on people because she was a sometimes unpleasant person, or because she was manipulating psychology for their own benefit, the result was the same. After all, the greatest cruelty would have been for her to let them settle into a comfortable mediocrity.

If Vengerova had annihilated me immediately after announcing that the honeymoon was over, it would have been possible to suspect her sincerity. Instead, she fed me still more rope, along with a compliment or two, and let me hang myself. I came for my eighth music lesson quite tired, after several nights of short sleep, and with a wretchedly prepared assignment. With other teachers such misbehavior had been punished by varying degrees of verbal wrist-slaps, and I had escaped by putting on a solemn face to promise that I would "work harder next week." This was my first bad lesson for Mme. Vengerova, though, and I was distinctly off-balance. Lack of sleep rendered my mind more susceptible to strong impressions.

I was just the way she wanted me.

Madame studied me quietly for a moment before the lesson began. I think she knew this was the day. "Play," she ordered, without preamble. I began playing as she seated herself heavily at the second of the two large pianos in her studio. Three and a half measures later, I heard her hand rapping softly on the fall board of her instrument.

"Harry," she always rolled the "r's" slightly, "I want to talk with you. Are you ill?" she asked.

In spite of our different backgrounds, my wife and I found happiness in one purpose and one way of life.

Photo by Fisher Neal

Courtesy of Australian Broadcasting Commission

Allison was a child prodigy. I was not.

photos by Benjamin Spiegel
s otherwise credited

Nashville Tennessean

In Paris, Tennessee, *we bought a big white elephant, a small green truck, and two pianos. Soon our homemade concert tours were covering the country. Later we acquired Neal's Folly, a perfidious custom coach with living quarters for eight.*

On the road, people say: "Of course you live in New York?"
Why should we live in a big city when Paris, Tennessee,
has the same advantages?

Crowds?

Music shops?

The symphony?

The thrill of big-league sports?

"Why don't you leave your children at home?" they always ask.

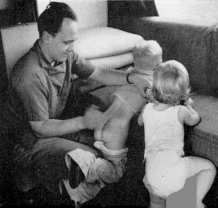

The answer is found in those precious everyday moments: What would you trade for a little girl's sudden gesture of affection? Who can comfort a little boy better than his mother, or straighten him out quicker than his father? Who would miss the wonder of his son's dreaming out of the window, or that goodnight kiss every single night?

Nighttime is concert time. And concerts mean many things.

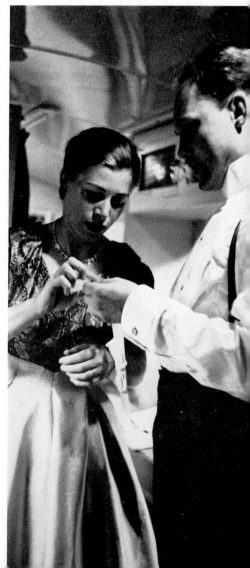

For our little girl — stealing a sly peep as we dress (she's supposed to be asleep) — concerts mean excitement and glitter.

Spiegel photo, courtesy of Cities Service Company

For her parents, these nights mean an exact schedule, ending with two hours of intense dedication. Supper is at 5:45. Allison washes the dishes while I get the children to bed at 6:30. We nap at 7:00; dress at 7:40; concerts are usually at 8:15.

Once on stage, the world seems to fall away from us. We are alone with the music and God. It is for these moments that we live.

But all is not serious. I enjoy teasing the audience during encores.

Wave As You Pass!

I had rehearsed answers to everything I thought she might say, but this oblique attack caught me so flat-footed that I only shook my head. Whatever agility youth is supposed to have, it never offered me any aid in coping with that quick and wily mind of hers. On the offensive, she never continued a single attack long enough for her victim to gather his resources and prepare an answer; I can never recall her saying what I expected or hoped.

"Too bad. I had hoped that you were ill." With a long sigh, she traced a silent melody on her keyboard. "I always make allowances when my students do not feel well. But you . . . you just did not practice." Her voice was so low as to seem almost offhand.

"Now let us have an understanding." There was nothing offhand in her voice now. "In this studio, at the Curtis, one does not make mistakes. You cannot play wrong notes for me." (What a stunning pronouncement! I had always thought right notes to be a matter of talent and luck, rather beyond the player's conscious control.) "Perhaps—once in a great while—a finger slips, but you do not play wrong notes. Rather than bring such a lesson before me, you should have called up the school and said that you were sick—that you were ill—and have hidden your shame at home. Then at least I might have been able to give this time to someone who had worked and needed the help."

I was amazed that she knew so much about my lesson from such a small sample. I thought those three and a half measures had been all right, for we hadn't even begun to reach the place where it was really bad!

"I'm an old woman, Harry—" again the curious roll of the "r's"— "and have not many good years left. You should be trying to soak up knowledge from me as a sponge takes up water. Yet you let the days go by. . . ." Her voice trailed off in sadness.

"I had a gifted pupil once, and mentioned his talent to Rachmaninoff . . . you have heard of Rachmaninoff? . . . his only answer was, 'Yes, so God gave the boy talent, but does he practice?' You do not practice, and without practice you have nothing.

"You, my boy, are eighteen years old and have a pianistic age of only about twelve. You should be trying desperately hard to raise it to at least fifteen by the end of this year." Always the stately roll of her voice added a strange emphasis to her words. "You must learn how to learn, and stop wasting our valuable time on fundamentals. You struggle note for note through the music, while others file away scales, chords, *arpeggios*, and all such technical tools, each in a separate drawer. Then, when they look at the music, they recognize the pattern, open the drawer, and there is the skill they need."

I was like putty in her hands. A simple tirade would have raised all my defenses; in such cases we usually bow our figurative heads, unhearing, and wait for the storm to subside. As it was, she had maneuvered me into listening intently to every word she uttered. She awed me by comparing my lessons to those of other students, which consisted of "possibly a few minor corrections in fingering, a couple of finger exercises on a difficult spot or two, and the rest on interpretation."

An outsider might have considered that this was at variance with some of the tales I had heard, but my mind was eagerly following hers in complete confidence and vulnerability. At this point she moved into her real offensive.

Suddenly, brutally, as no one had ever done before, she was laying out my character for open inspection. I was lazy. I was spoiled. I was conceited. I felt sorry for myself. While admitting my ignorance, I was seeking to trade on the sympathy it aroused at Curtis, rather than producing great quantities of superior work. In my present state of development, even when trying hardest, I would play a few notes well, the next badly, then well, and so forth. My concentration was poor; four and a half hours' practice from me sounded like half that time from a good student. Therefore I needed to work even harder than everyone else.

On and on she swept.

"You have a frightful tendency toward amateurishness. At first there was the natural ability to do any one of many things well; this resulted not in your concentrating, so as to do one thing very well, but in your doing many things halfway well; that resulted in your being praised to high heaven and told you had 'great possibilities' by people who knew nothing. Do you know that Schumann said there was no worse fate than to be praised by rascals?

"In all your life you have never realized your possibilities. You never will, as long as you live, unless you completely change your way of thinking and living. And if you don't neither I nor this institution have any use for you."

Fear had arrived.

Cold fear, the sweat-on-the-palms fear, the waking up in the night fear. Fear of one's self, of truth, of public humiliation, and failure. This woman had the power to dismiss me from Curtis at any time, for such are the rules of the school. Such an event, I was sure, would mean the end of music in my life. My hands began to shake slightly, and I clasped them together between my legs so that she might not notice.

"It seems to have escaped your notice, but I can tell anything from your playing. I can tell if you practiced every day, if you missed one day or two, and usually I can tell you which day it was that you missed. I can tell if you are in a good mental state. Indeed, I can make surprising observations about your personal life from your playing. Let me tell you about your room, as it looks at this very moment. . . ."

I could not believe my ears. Horror-stricken, I listened as she who had never seen my living quarters described them as though from a photograph. She spoke of an unmade bed, of newspapers on the floor, pictures hanging crooked on the wall, of music and clothes lying about, and even of dust on the piano. "An unforgivable sin. Mr. Serkin has such reverence for his instrument that he would never even place his hat on it! There is disorder in your mind, Harry. I hear it in your music, and I know it is in the rest of your life as well!"

The wrath of God is terrible because from it there is no refuge. Not only are one's actions open to scrutiny, but there is no tiniest corner of the mind which is inviolable. Vengerova chilled me with the fear that I could not hide my innermost thoughts from her, even after she had gone back to New York.

In retrospect, I can see a certain comic element in my panic. All my life I had heard music referred to as a medium of "communication," of its having "messages," of artists "speaking through their music," and so on. Suddenly I was stricken by the so-real fear that every time I sat down to play I was broadcasting messages to all and sundry about my dirty underwear!

It was not amusing at the time.

Numbly I listened as she told me of the exactitude required of a professional artist. Bringing about a good musical performance required more intricate and exact work, she said, than creating the finest Swiss watch. "Since art is a marvelous—or merciless, as the case may be—mirror of the personality, you must be exact in everything, if you would be exact in music.

"Go home, and never let me speak to you in anger again."

I was dismissed.

There was no walk down the stairs together. She waited until I had left the room for a safe period. Only then did she whom I worshiped as a demigod open the door to descend the stairs alone and uncontaminated.

Depriving me of our after-lesson walk was the first move in cutting away all those little special attentions which had come to mean so much. Next day, I was called into the office and informed that I was needing so much time for practice that Mme. Vengerova would understand when I did not meet her train in the future.

I went home and wept.

There is an old saying among musicians which can completely change a student's point of view about learning his instrument: "Technique is not in the fingers, but in the mind."

The layman tends to forget that it is his mind or nervous system, and not the muscle tissue itself which one is trying to train by practice. In order to improve my technical pianism, Vengerova felt it necessary to remake my entire life, from the nervous system outwards.

She did. Even today I scurry about cleaning up my living quarters, with the gentle rasp of her voice still sounding in my ears.

There are no fires in hell; no pits of molten lava; no demons. The punishment of hell is to be cut off from the love of God. This Vengerova had done to me.

What else could she have done which would have excited me to such a lifetime of effort? Now, long after her death, I am still trying to win my way back into her favor. At first, though, the eccentricities of human nature made it almost impossible for me to go to the piano. The shock was such that my work became even more erratic. I would sit and look at the piano for long periods, unable to put my hands on the keyboard. I alternately worked feverishly and neglected the instrument altogether.

But a birth process was beginning, and from it would come a new life.

The following week, Vengerova announced that I must be ill, whether I knew it or not, and sent me to a doctor of her choosing. He found that my eyes did not focus properly, that I had anemia, and a low-thyroid condition. Triumphantly she ordered me to undergo treatment for these defects.

Picking up my cold hand she asked, "Why are you afraid of me? No one else is!"

Strangely, I did not seem to be afraid. In a curiously detached way I knew that my heart was pounding, my hands shaking and my mind going blank. But this was all unreal, as though I were a third person watching a dreadful play. It was only my body that was afraid. It was only that *machine* of mine which seemed so afraid, and so out of control.

"You seem pale," she mused. Joe Rezits and I chipped in to buy a sun lamp and showed up for our next lessons so burned that we could hardly button our collars. Was there a smile in her voice when she said, "Much better"?

"Harry," cried Mme. Vengerova one day, "is it possible that I am fifty years older than you and yet have better hearing? Do you hear it when your fingers slip? Show me some sign! Give a grunt, or a nod of the head, or say, 'excuse me'! Otherwise I think you are unaware, and I have to stop you to point it out."

I took to saying, "Pardon me." I "pardoned me" up the scale and "pardoned me" down. Finally Madame could stand it no longer. "Ask Beethoven's pardon, not mine."

Curtis furnished free tickets to all concerts, and I found watching the other students almost as interesting as listening to the performing artists. We all sat in a box together, where one might be observed with his nose buried in a score; another would be conducting away furiously as though on the podium himself; someone else's hands might be playing along with the soloist, carefully creating the impression that he knew the score so well that such motions must come involuntarily when he heard the music. This boy sings to himself, making sure it is loud enough to attract the attention of everyone nearby. That girl smiles at certain passages, another frowns; there are soulful faces, agonized faces, disdainful faces, worshipful faces.

There are knowing chuckles when a difficult passage doesn't come off cleanly, and always loudly voiced criticisms. One boy asks another for an opinion, then races to a third, loudly proclaiming it as his own. Another leans from side to side taking a poll of the rest, so he will know what to say he thinks of the music. At times their eternal contortions made me feel I had wandered into a sort of comic Inferno full of writhing lost souls. These people never heard any ordinary music. It was always "fantastic," or "tremendous," or "fabulous," or sometimes just "astounding." Otherwise it was plain terrible. There was no in between.

To them, an artist seldom played well unless he had taught or studied at the Curtis Institute. One day I asked Madame about their fierce criticism of visiting recitalists.

Drily she quoted Chekov. "One does not become a saint through other people's sins."

Perhaps I can take credit for one good decision which was in distinct contrast to the lack of moderation in the students about me. I made a resolution to refrain from uttering a single musical opinion of mine during my entire first year at Curtis, on the grounds of complete ignorance. It was one of the few resolutions which I kept scrupulously, and I still think of it with approval. He seldom seems the fool who has his mouth shut and his ears open.

Almost everything else seemed wrong.

I can remember playing, eyes glued to the keyboard, and aware of Vengerova seated in her chair at the other piano. What an agony it was to continue playing when she rose with anger to come and stand over me! My fingers would tremble and my mouth go dry, so that my tongue continually flicked on my lips. Sometimes I would get frightful cramps in the small of my back at such moments; still, one had to keep playing. My phrases would become bumpy and it was almost a relief when the inevitable breakdown came.

"You must be very talented to play this way. In spite of all my experience, I could not possibly play if my wrist were as stiff as yours. Would you teach me how to accomplish this miracle?"

If some weeks I practiced five or six hours every day: "It is better today. You worked a little, but you must work more yet. I had to stop too often for explanations. I wish better lessons yet."

At one lesson I played a couple of works quite well, and she was encouraged to give me a talk urging a supreme effort to attain real perfectionism. "Let not the tiniest flaw slip from underneath your fingers. Exactness in everything is of the greatest importance!"

The next piece, of which I felt quite sure, was terrible. Just terrible. Madame ordered, "Again!" and it was almost as bad. "Again!" she commanded, and I showed some improvement. "Again!" This time it was fairly presentable. Standing up at her piano, she cried, "Now that you can remember it, make music of it instead of a finger exercise!" Once again I battled the demons.

"The first time you played this piece," she rasped, "I was so furious that I had to pace the floor, but I told myself, 'Surely this is wrong; he cannot possibly be this bad.' So I had you play it over and over until you regained your poise and were able to play it as rehearsed." From there she went on to urge the development of character, self-control and poise. "Next time you walk in that door, you must very properly be a man of iron!"

Tirelessly, that seventy-year-old powerhouse sought for psychological weaknesses with which she could goad me into greater efforts. I showed her a beautiful letter from my father; thinking that might be the key, she began pleading with me not to disgrace my family by failure. Until learning that race meant nothing to me, she tried to trade on my Southern background and infuriate me into activity by describing how much better one of her colored pupils was progressing than I.

My practice was still erratic but improvement did take place. One day Madame smiled. "Not bad. You are better. Now at last we are ready to do some real refinements; you must now try to attain a new level of work."

What, again? I thought.

The next ten or fifteen minutes were spent on about a half line of music. Every note had a hitherto-unheard-of purpose. This note had this relation to that note. Together they had a certain relationship to still others. Deeper and deeper we went, until I completely lost track of it all. Suddenly Vengerova laughed. "I am always amused by the bewilderment of beginners when they are faced with all these new problems!" Really, she was quite merry. After laughing and joking with me to ease the tension, she tore back into the music.

It was one of those lessons which give you hope.

In New York, that week end, I played for Howard Rothschild, the friend who had originally encouraged me to leave Paris, Tennessee. Howard was not pleased with my progress and visited Madame personally to ask for an accounting. At my next lesson, she was furious. "How dare you play for someone without my knowledge and permission? Do you imagine that in your present confused state you are qualified to make music?" As I crept out of the studio she said softly, "This Rothschild, he likes you. But then he does not know you very well, does he?"

In the following lessons, her manner took a more biting turn.

"See," she would ask acidly, "if you can keep me from having to repeat this more than . . . ten times, at least!"

"Are you lazy or conceited—or just stupid?"

I opened the door at the end of a lesson. Waiting until the new pupil walked in she called out, "You have made an utter fool of yourself."

Jacob Lateiner and I were what Madame considered her two black-with-laziness sheep. (Although Madame always admitted that Jacob could play marvelously. "Like a god," was her expression.) During the Christmas holidays we were called to New York for lessons with lectures attached. Jacob never volunteered an account of his session, beyond the observation that it "wasn't too bad." After I went in for my scourging, Madame made me comfortable and started to work on my laziness in earnest.

"How much do you practice? . . . Why not more? . . . You feel you are too busy. Very well, describe a typical day to me. What time do you get up? . . . Then what do you do? . . . And after breakfast? . . ." On and on she plunged, tearing great holes in the thin fabric of what I claimed was my schedule for the day. After an embarrassing defense of weak excuses on my part, I heard her sum up what was clearly the truth.

"The real answer to this mystery is simply that you are lazy, and you will offer any ridiculous excuse rather than look that word in the face.

"You have accustomed yourself to living with the excuse that you will do everything 'tomorrow.' You must tear that word out by the roots and fight 'today' or die. You are in Yankee-land now, Harry, and we are not easygoing." (How strange those words sounded in her thick, rolling accent!) "I am Rosh-ian, and you *know we* are not easygoing."

"I have beaten this philosophy into others, and I shall beat it into you!"

Practice!

"You are a stubborn boy, Harry, but I also am stubborn. I will not let you waste yourself."

Practice!

"Remember, the greater the artist, the longer the phrase line."

Practice!

"Don't *crescendo* so soon! A real artist always saves his climax as long as possible."

Practice!

"You have to learn not to waste yourself on stops! Every day must see something new accomplished. Every moment you live is gone forever, never to return!"

Practice!

"But, Madame, I *did* practice!"

"You lie to me!"

"I'm not a liar," I lied.

"The wicked flee when no man pursueth."

After each of those dreadful ordeals with Vengerova, no thought consumed me as much as the desire to hide. No longer did I yearn for those post-lesson walks together. The moment her door closed behind me I surrendered myself to an ecstasy of flight.

If the lesson had been good, of course, I paraded proudly down the massive stairway, admiring the high-ceilinged "common room" which was our entrance hall at Curtis. If it had been bad, I slipped instead down a side hall to the fire escape, made my way down it to the basement, and left the school through a long dark passageway which emptied into an alley behind the recital hall. For some reason, I had a mortal dread of being seen. Even after leaving by that circuitous route I would walk still further, all the way around the block, rather than pass the Locust Street window of the school secretary.

It was early 1947, and on this day I had crept like a whipped puppy down the hall to the large deserted corner studio in which my audition had been held almost a year before. Mrs. Zimbalist, who as Mary Curtis Bok had founded the Institute a quarter of a century before, had listened to my audition in the comfortable overstuffed chair which I now occupied. Gazing at the large piano, I relived my audition again. I watched the comedy of errors over removing my coat, I heard my flounder in the Bach, and once again I heard my questions to the jurors.

If there were limits to how good I could become, I had said, I didn't want to continue the piano. Why then this weekly torture? If she didn't want me, why didn't she say so at the beginning? It seemed terribly unfair. I was enjoying what Vengerova so often described as my favorite sport: I was feeling sorry for myself.

Suddenly the door burst open and a slim young girl stepped inside. She was one of Mr. Serkin's students, and wanted to practice. I stayed and listened while she worked on the Brahms *F-minor Sonata*. A few weeks before, having heard that she and Seymour Lipkin were no longer dating one another, I had taken her to supper.

Since then she had returned again and again to my mind. I must have been doing what Dad used to call "noticing" her, for I can remember running into her frequently after that first date. I seemed always to be chancing into rooms where she was practicing. When her escort became drunk at a rowdy party, I helped her take him home. On the excuse that we were waiting until he was all right, we sat together reading St. Exupéry's *Le Petit Prince*. As we smiled together while she read that wistful little tale, I began to look carefully at Allison Nelson.

I watched her eyes, which had seemed so sad since she and Seymour had broken up. Her small, muscular body was somehow tense and nervous, and I looked at her hair, her regular little nose (which looked so well on stage) and perfect teeth. Her pleasant Australian accent seemed just exotic enough to unsettle my nervous system. I wanted very much to kiss her then, but I was not quite so bold as I made out to Joe Rezits.

A few nights later, I noticed her among a group of students Abba Bogin had invited over to his room. What an exciting night that was!

The next day Abba was to play in the Naumberg contest, which gave the winner a New York Town Hall debut recital. This was exciting enough, but what made the air crackle with tension was that his last lesson with Vengerova had been a disastrous one, and she had absolutely forbidden his playing in that contest. Although Abba had been studying with Madame since the age of four, this was an offense for which he might be thrown out of school. Personal rebellion was one thing Vengerova would not endure.

Once entering, Abba's only hope was to win, for then she could not very well be angry.

How he played for us that night! Can anyone ever play again the way they have played for you in memory? With all of us seated on the chairs, the bed, and the floor, with cigarette smoke hanging heavy in the air, with a single light burning over his piano, Abba played and played and played. You may have all your concerts and crowds; this was real music-making: playing your heart away for people who understood what you were doing and loved it and loved you for it.

Every time he stopped there would come an excited clamor: "Wonderful! . . . A little more sharply on the peak of that phrase . . . *non legato* here . . . oh, Abba, you sound so sexy! (drop around some time) . . . Play the Schubert next . . ." I listened while they schemed and plotted: "The last movement here is the weakest in your whole contest repertoire. What if they ask you to play it? Why not walk right in and play the first movement immediately as the work of your choice? They'd be sure to ask for other works when you got through, and it would trick them out of ever hearing the end of the Schubert!"

At Latin-American universities, students may try to convince themselves of dawning maturity by attending and plotting at revolutionary political rallies. At Curtis we were infinitely more daring: we plotted rebellion to Mme. Vengerova. Those other students risked a mere political prison or firing squad. We, on the other hand, were risking the wrath of Isabelle Vengerova!

Abba won his contest, and his daring gave courage to others. When Joe Rezits had his last lesson before the Philadelphia Orchestra's Youth Contest, Madame also forbade him to play. He played, risking everything, and won. It must have been hard for her.

I was very conscious of Allison that night, and tried to maneuver my way into taking her home. A bassoonist beat me to it, and it was a long time before I had any use for bassoonists. On March 7, 1947, I took Allison to hear a recital by Mieczyslaw Horszowski. The recital was a revelation. I had come to look on Horszowski as just "Mr. Serkin's assistant" and had always believed that no man was a great artist unless he had a full-page picture in the *Musical America* annual downstairs. Yet here was a man almost unknown in this country, a strange, tiny, shy man whose music was magical, and in whose soul was greatness.

Did I really fall in love with Allison that night? Or was my heart bewitched through my ears, as Mephisto had bewitched the villagers for Faust?

Whatever it was, from that moment forward Allison and I were inseparable.

There are many false ideas about music and musicians. Often these ideas are fostered by musicians themselves for purposes of self-advancement. At this point I would love to tell you that I was like Alexander the Great, who profited from every mistake, and seldom made the same error twice.

Alas, it was not so.

My late nights the previous fall, and their disastrous consequences, seemed to have taught me nothing at all. Any time we were not in separate classes, Allison and I could be found together. We had lunch together, we had supper together, we went to concerts together, we studied together, we went to dances together, and even the smelly old Schuylkill River's bank seemed a romantic garden to our starlit eyes. We dated almost every single night, staying up until hours which today make me feel like a very old man.

Immediately we had the first of many arguments about music, and it was a hot one. I was primarily an instinctive pianist (which is to say that I seldom used my head) and Allison was a distinctly intellectual musician. When we found a middle ground between the two it made us become together much more than the sum of our separate selves would ever have been.

How well I remember that first argument! We were at a YMCA dance; hardly had we gotten on the floor than we were arguing heatedly about the lengths to which one could go for romantic effects while performing. We left the dance and marched home to get a piano with which to prove our respective points. When it came my turn I played a passage from the Chopin *Nocturne in E minor* (Posthumous), which I had learned from Dorsey Whittington. Whittington was a crafty romanticist, and there was one place near the end where he always distorted the rhythm slightly in such a sensuous manner that it invariably gave me an almost erotic twinge in the solar plexus; when I reached that point I imitated his playing exactly: Allison gave a self-conscious giggle!

"There, you see? I tell you it's good to schmaltz up a place like that!"

Somehow the argument could not be settled.

I carried my point to Mme. Vengerova, and was so excited about the music that I forgot to be afraid of her. "That is very interesting, what you do," she said, "but let me caution you again that 'the greater the artist, the longer his phrase line.' One must be very careful. To halt a phrase line continually for such devices would be immature. But once in a while . . .

"You know, this thing you do is almost immoral. It's indecent. Did someone put you up to it? Abba Bogin, perhaps?"

In spite of my late nights, I was suddenly having my best lessons of the year. "How can you expect to have good lessons when you practice hard one week and do nothing the next?" demanded Allison. The fact that she was a girl made me believe her.

Madame no longer seemed quite so ferocious, but it was still impossible to satisfy her. Almost never would she let me leave her studio without that curious feeling of frustration which kept her students working so hard.

"I'll try to have a really good lesson for you next week, Madame."

"Really? But we are not doing this for me, Harry. It is for you that we struggle."

Let me tell her how much I had loved my lessons with Olga Stroumillo, her assistant, and Madame would reply, "Yes, but Miss Stroumillo tells me that you are such a difficult pupil that she had to lie down for an hour after each of your lessons."

Nothing could ever dampen my enthusiasm over those occasional lessons with Stroumillo. Charming, filled with buoyant enthusiasm, she hammered away at my heathenish laziness, and often said things which were to serve as beacon lights for me in the future. I remember her saying, "I won't say anything about practicing this very day, because that might upset you. But just think: if you had practiced four hours every day last year, think how glad you would be of it today!

"Remember, you must practice today for all the tomorrows yet to come! Get out of bed every morning hardly able to wait until you can reach your piano!"

On Easter Sunday, Allison invited me to dinner at the home of Mr. and Mrs. Sydney L. Wright, who lived just outside of Philadelphia. The Wrights had met Allison through Mr. Ormandy and promptly made her a member of their family. There was no kindness which they did not shower upon her, and when Allison's older sister Kathleen came over from Australia to live with her, the Wrights practically adopted both of them. Their home, Endsmeet Farm, furnished the Nelson girls with a haven from the bustle of the city almost every week end and holiday.

It was important to Allison that the Wrights like me.

I was terribly nervous. I wanted to make good with the Wrights particularly, because Allison's sister Kathleen was beginning to disapprove of me. She had been sent over from Australia to "look after" Allison, and perhaps keep her out of trouble. Allison felt she did not need looking after but Kathie could see that I was fast becoming what George Washington would have described as an "entangling alliance." Indeed I was.

My main recollection of that dinner at the Wrights is that I could think of nothing to say beyond, "Ah, me!" They seated me at a table beside Edna Phillips, the harpist. Did I have a nice trip out from town? "Ah, me!" Isn't it a lovely day? "Ah, me!" May I have some butter, please? "Ah, me!" Would you look at that dessert! "Ah, me!" I ah-me'd short and I ah-me'd long. There were brisk ones and lazy ones, I sighed it and I blurted it, and in all that meal I can hardly remember saying ten other words.

Yes, I did say something else. After dinner we were all out on the lawn and I tried to interest Syd by saying that I had spent the Christmas holidays with the James Bush-Browns whom he might know. "Yes," he muttered, studying a cloud, "they always were gluttons for punishment."

I suspected I had not made the grade.

But I had Allison, and with her help and encouragement, it seemed much easier to practice than before. Once she saw me begin to move in this direction, Madame Vengerova pressed even harder than before. She ordered me to listen to other students' lessons. I recall her telling Abba Bogin for my benefit, "One does not play because one is 'in the mood.' A musician plies his craft at any time, the same as everyone else." Later she told me an anecdote about Tchaikovsky, who began composing at precisely the same time every morning. But what did he do, some maidenly ladies wanted to know, if the muses did not inspire him at that particular moment? "Mesdames les Muses," he glowered, "have learned to be on time for my appointments!"

Before I knew it, the year was over. Allison was happy because she had just been awarded the Curtis Alumni prize, designating her as the best student in school that year; as for me, "Have a good last lesson," Joe had urged, "and Madame will be sure to keep you next year."

Mme. Vengerova was pleased. "Don't drop into bad work habits over the summer. This is a bad time in your development for you to be away from me. You are 'catching on' but you play neither your old way, nor my new one. My friend, you are in the position of being neither a Christian nor a heathen; you are just very well befuddled!"

To my amazement, she got me a summer job. "The sun will do you good," she laughed, and off she shipped me to be music counselor at a boys' camp in Maine. As I got on the train I could still hear her exasperated voice, from one of my last lessons:

"What do you want of me? That I should pamper your little ego? No! For you my studio is a jungle, and in it you must fight for your life. Stand up like a man and I'll goad you, and I'll drive you, and I'll torment you until you grow into more than you know!"

The summer of 1947 marked the point at which I began to see pianistic daylight, far in the future. It also marked the beginning of the end for Vengerova and me.

I entrained for Camp Belgrade with original, unedited editions of the Mozart and Beethoven sonatas under my arm. Allison had given me those editions (to which Vengerova objected so heartily) with instructions to sight-read from them all summer. Up to that point my sight-reading had been utterly impossible. I would see a note in the music, look down to find it on the keyboard, look up again, down, up and down. When I got to the middle of the page it would become harder and harder to find my place in the music, with my corresponding lag at the keyboard becoming more and more excruciating. I resembled nothing so much as one of those toy men whom you wind up so that their heads will bob up and down like little maniacs.

Allison's advice had been to stop worrying self-consciously about a "method" and just try to play the piano again. I was to practice percussively, and work my fingers as hard as possible. Vengerova had accused me of disobediance and rebelliousness many times, but working percussively on those unedited editions of the Mozart and Beethoven was the first thing I had ever done in deliberate disregard of her wishes.

At camp that summer I read all those sonatas through twice, in addition to working on my regular repertoire. Some of Vengerova's fire-eating seemed to be paying off, too, for I practiced regularly. Stroumillo's voice became the alarm which awakened me every morning: "Get out of bed hardly able to wait to start practicing!" I would hear. Sure enough, I'd jump up, run to that wretched camp piano, and do a good day's practice before it was time for work. The effects of the practice recommended by Allison were remarkable. When I got back to school, Madame pronounced my hands and playing so "much improved" that she felt sure we would get along "much better this time."

She had told me to stand up like a man. I had decided upon a course of action, and even though it was contrary to her wishes, I had done it. She approved of the results without knowing how I had gotten them. That seemed enough for me. From then on I meant to be a free agent.

It did not take Vengerova long to find out.

Madame's practice, when ready to assign me a new work, had been to give a quick lesson on some piece I was finishing, and say suddenly, "Now what else have you to play for me?" Since she had assigned nothing, I would have nothing. She would then moan about what was to become of me, finish the lesson on the work we had just gotten through with, and proceed to assign whatever she had intended that I study next.

I began trying to stay ahead of her. I worked on new pieces at home, and at these lessons would reach proudly into my music, drag forth a new work, and perform it for her. In this manner I hoped to impress her with my industry, and it also gave me a chance to choose the next field on which we were to do battle. First, I brought in Scarlatti; Allison had persuaded me to play certain places in it *non legato* on the grounds that Scarlatti's instrument could not sustain a tone long enough to achieve the smooth, connected *legato* available on today's instruments. This could be justified musically on the grounds that Scarlatti's musical thoughts were in terms of the instrument at his disposal.

Disaster.

A beautiful, singing *legato* was one of those things on which Vengerova prided herself most. Playing *non legato* (with a break between each note) was heresy to her unless such an attack was specifically indicated in the music. But Scarlatti himself had written no phrase markings at all, either *legato* or *non legato*. I maintained one had to decide those things for himself (with the help of his girl friend!).

Madame wound up in her best honeymoon-is-over style, and breathed fire all over me. She insisted that composers often thought well beyond the possibilities of the instrument at their disposal. Beethoven had written a *crescendo* over a single chord in one of his sonatas, anticipating a possibility not yet available even on present-day pianos. "And besides," she snorted, "we are not bound by the past. We no longer castrate little boys in order to make sopranos; we simply use girls!"

The cat was out of the bag. She knew I was beginning to try out ideas of my own regardless of the consequences. She could not be the great teacher she was without a certain fanaticism, and one thing she was a fanatic about was absolute obedience. Immediately she bent every effort to stamp out my heretical tendencies. "I am sure Dr. Whittington was a fine teacher; yet I can imagine how your lessons with him would go. He would give you his opinion, and then—although this places an uncomfortable burden upon my imagination—perhaps you gave him your ideas. You would discuss

things and each would leave with the same ideas. Here you do
it my way!"

The previous year Madame had assigned the Beethoven *Sonata
Opus 2 No. 2, in A major*. In all my experience before, two or
three pages had been enough to prepare for a new lesson; for
Vengerova, I shot the works and got the whole first movement,
memorized and up to the tempo.

She was shocked. "Only one movement? In four hours a day,
Harry, you should have prepared two whole sonatas for me!"

Later I have suspected she was not nearly so shocked as she
pretended, but that she must undoubtedly have considered that
the proper move at the proper time. This year I left nothing to
chance, and every work I brought for her was memorized and up
to the tempo before she heard it. In the case of a Beethoven
sonata this meant about ten times the amount of preparation I
brought my teachers before her. It is possible that there was method
in her madness.

Next I brought in the Beethoven *Sonata in E-flat, Opus 31 No. 3*,
which I had been wanting to study for some time. Instead of seeming happy over my newly industrious habits, she wanted to know,
"What do you mean, bringing such a difficult work to me? Do you
imagine that you are so advanced that you can order your own
destiny? This is a work such as my advanced pupils might bring
in, but not you. Yet, I suppose I mustn't let your efforts be entirely
wasted; I will teach it to you. Play."

Trying to tone myself down a bit, I next produced the famous
Bach *Prelude and Fugue in C major*. She consented to hear this
work, and I assumed it was correct to begin at the beginning. I
started the prelude. "How dare you play this kindergarten piece
for me? I want no tinkling finger exercises, I want music! Play
the fugue." I simply did not know what to think.

Everything I did seemed an exaggeration of her instructions. It
was either too much or too little. "Harry, you must practice more
slowly. You young people never believe it, but practicing slowly
is the quickest way to learn." All the next week I practiced slowly
enough to drive my landlady half crazy. Then, "What is the matter?
Why can you not play up to the tempo? You do nothing but
practice slowly all week, and then expect some miracle to happen
on Wednesday morning!"

Trying to maintain what I understood was the correct hand position, I had trouble reaching part of a chord with the thumb of my left hand. "Turn your hand! Turn your hand on an angle, so your thumb can reach that note! By the gods, you have no sense at all. Most of my pupils do these things instinctively, without being told."

"What is the matter?" she asked one day. "Can you not see how this development works? Beethoven takes this part of the theme, and repeats it so . . . and so . . . and so." Her words were like illuminating shafts of sunlight. Something else must have happened during that lesson to render me susceptible, for I remember a great thrill, and a feeling of intense elation over discovery of the development she was outlining. Suddenly, I was dashed to the ground when I heard her snort, "This is so boring!"

One day when she assured me that it was quite impossible to produce a good sound with percussive playing, I asked a question which had troubled me more and more. "Madame, I heard Mr. Serkin play last night, and although he played percussively I thought his tone was perfectly beautiful . . . I don't understand."

I now know it was the wrong thing to say. She could not attack me without at least implying a criticism of Mr. Serkin, who was head of the piano department. She eyed me silently for a long time. Finally she said coldly, "When you play like Mr. Serkin, I will say nothing further to you about piano technique."

The following week a most dreadful scene occurred. Madame had disagreed with some phrasing and asked from which of my spurious editions I had collected *that* fantasy. I replied that it was from Breitkopf and Härtel. My attempted German pronunciation must have been atrocious for she assured me there was no such edition. We had a sharp disagreement which ended with her branding me a liar. Whatever I might be, I was no longer lying to Isabelle Vengerova. Smarting furiously under her accusations, I brought the offending edition to my next lesson to prove that it and the phrase line existed just as I had said.

"What? What is this? Do you dare to defy me openly? This cannot be endured!" A torrent of abuse stormed out of her, and she spoke with such agitation that a small froth of saliva began to form at one corner of her mouth and slowly dribbled down to her chin. I could hardly hear what she was saying for the wonderment of watching that saliva. I remember wondering if this was what you called "frothing at the mouth." Whatever it was, I had no further comments to make about Messrs. Breitkopf and Härtel.

An impossibly bitter atmosphere began to invade our lessons. Many of Madame's observations seemed to be losing the exquisite control with which she had goaded me the previous year. My tentative impression is that the thought of losing control of me was so infuriating to Vengerova that she began losing control of herself. Her attitude seemed to deteriorate into personal hostility.

Memory fades into a haze in which biting remarks float at random.

"You have a nice voice; could you learn to sing?" Another time, "Would you like to study with Mr. Horszowski?" And often, "I simply cannot understand you!"

Do you remember playing hide-and-seek as a child and being convinced that the child playing "it" would find you because your heart was beating so loudly? I remember being reduced to terror at one of those lessons, and having the irrational conviction that Vengerova was just about to assault me again because my heart was beating so loudly, and *out of time with the music.*

Madame had a new pupil this year, Anthony di Bonaventura (whose marriage to Kate Whitney later attracted much attention). Joe tried to console me by saying that he had seen Tony coming down from a lesson looking as white as though he had been dead for six hours. But I was beyond being consoled by other people's miseries.

"You are not so clever as I thought" . . . "You are a child, really" . . . "Sit still! That piano stool is not a garden swing!" . . . "Now pull yourself together and see if you can *think,* just a little bit!"

One, two, three, four, five, six, seven days, and the weekly crucifixion had arrived again. I was like an animal dazed by the lights of an automobile, not knowing which way to run, and freezing still in the path of oncoming destruction.

"Why don't you become an actor? It doesn't take much talent."

Vengerova's studio was a jungle, and I was fighting for my life. Troubles with her were compounded by the fact that they made

Allison's family all the more suspicious of me. I was desperate. It seemed absolutely necessary to prove myself in some way. Luckily, I hit upon a solution which helped my cause with Allison, if not with Madame Vengerova.

Kathie had told Allison that instead of me, she should be interesting herself in someone who had the money to finance a concert career. Allison's sister had thus unwittingly furnished us with the one last thing we needed to bind us together: we had an ogre to hide from together and to plot against. This ogre had made a move against me. My counter move surprised us all with its success.

I enlisted my mother's aid in writing schools and music clubs in the vicinity of Paris, Tennessee, and secured a number of engagements for Allison at fees ranging from $50 to $100. Dwight Anderson, of the University of Louisville (the author of my "intellectual integrity" letter at Interlochen), took a strong interest and helped Mother in many ways. We shelled out $19.23 for a little advertising brochure, and the Nelson and Neal concert business was born.

Mother accepted no payment for her efforts, but even then Allison cleared only about $100 after expenses. Still, she had met my parents, which was important to us, and I had proved to her family that I could be some help in her career. My folks were enthusiastic. Dad's remarks were typical. About the music: "I didn't understand it, but you could tell it was class." And about my girl: "We Neals always did pick women smarter than we were."

My victory seemed compounded, just as the defeats had been. Allison's recitals created such a stir that no sooner did she get back to Philadelphia than a wire came offering $175 if she would return instantly for another concert in Union City, Tennessee. It was the first serious recital that city had ever had, and local enthusiasm was such that they then joined the Civic Concert Service and established a regular artist series in the community. We were on top of the world.

My standing seemed to rise in school, though Vengerova was unhappy that I had wasted these efforts on someone not in her piano class.

I needed money and was offered a job singing in a night-club quartet. Madame refused to allow it on the grounds that the environment would not be good. "You are a nice-looking boy. Women

would be the ruination of you." At this point she insisted that I
end my money troubles by allowing Howard Rothschild to help
me, as he had once generously offered to do. As a matter of pride,
I refused, even though she threatened to dismiss me from school
for "open rebellion."

My next brainstorm was to write a set of three one-act plays. I
planned to borrow enough money to produce them during the
summer. Of course it was a foregone conclusion that any plays
written by me would be an enormous success and would make so
much money that I would never have any troubles again. After I
had wasted a great deal of precious time writing the plays, securing
a little neighborhood theater and cast, and investigating publicity
outlets, Madame found out about it. I will spare the reader the
details of her reaction.

Finally, I tried to return to the concert-management idea, and
to curry favor by promoting one of Madame's pupils this time.
Night after night I stayed up laying out a promotion scheme to
sell Abba Bogin to the Lions Clubs of the northeastern U.S.A. Our
first success in Tennessee had been modest—something within our
reach; now, I set out boldly to conquer the Big Time.

If only I had known something about the concert business! Lions
Clubs, bless their souls, are interested in many things, but not in
concerts. Not long ago, I ran across one of the mailing pieces we
sent out in that campaign, and I was quite surprised to see what
an attractive little presentation we had prepared. It simply went
to the wrong people. We mailed 250 letters with proposals, bro-
chures on Abba, and stamped, self-addressed envelopes.

What a job it was! For three weeks every spare moment I could
find had been spent on the project. Even Allison's sister Kathie
became infected with the fever, and worked away folding letters
to help us. Allison had a severe stomach upset for three days as a
result of all the letter-licking. I printed a large supply of contracts
for our orders, and we waited for the mail to come rolling in.

In spite of all those self-addressed envelopes, only four replies
dribbled back to us. Three of those consisted of "Not interested"
scrawled across the original letter I had sent. Every day I met the
mailman a half block from our house. Every day I invented new
excuses why the letters were not forthcoming: the matter had to

wait for board meetings, or club meetings. But every day the mailman came empty-handed. Finally, I admitted that there would be
no replies. Our effort had been so great, and our hopes so high
that my misery was boundless. To make matters worse I had spent
nearly all of my living allowance on printing and postage. It was
a foolish gamble.

None of this escaped the all-seeing eye of Vengerova. The angrier she became, the worse I played. The worse I played, the
angrier she became. There was no stopping the cycle.

Suddenly, her attitude changed. It was as though a violent storm
had spent itself and its weary clouds quickly dispersed before a
fresh breeze and warming sun. No longer did she rage with fury
at my lessons. The struggle seemed over. Instead, she began telling
me things, earnestly entreating that I remember them. It was a
kind of teaching for which I thought I had been waiting.

We reviewed the techniques of efficient practice. She broke all
pianistic problems down into a series of tiny mundane jobs, each
understandable and drudge-like. Every technical problem was to
be hunted down to the point of its origin, which was usually one
or two notes in one hand or the other. "Time in life is so short,"
she said, "that you should not waste your time repeating notes you
already knew, as children do who start anew at the top of a page
after making mistakes on the fourth line."

Time and again she returned to principles which she urged that
I remember and carry with me always. "Brilliancy does not depend
on velocity but on clarity. What is not clear cannot scintillate nor
sparkle. Use your strongest fingers in brilliant passages, and hold
back. *Hold back*. Think of the tremendous excitement generated by
controlled 'holding back' such as one hears from an artist like
Horowitz!"

Distilling every thought for its essence, she laid out one principle
after another, always insisting that I commit them to memory.

"No! *Sforzando* does not always mean the same thing! It is
always kept in relation to the dynamic scale of the passage. *Sfz*
in a quiet passage is not nearly so loud as in a *forte* passage . . . To
make a good *crescendo*, begin more quietly; it allows a greater
climax at the end . . . Only a professional has nerve enough to
hold pauses long enough. Take time to breathe comfortably be-

tween phrases . . . Not so quickly! Amateurs are always ready to jump up from the piano at the conclusion of a piece. Sustain your mood. . . ."

Sometimes there would be flashes of the old fire and temper. Across the room, and with her back turned, she would flare, "I can hear you still putting your fifth finger on that B flat! Why do you not change it as I asked? . . . I don't know why I ever took you as a student. No, that is not true. There is no one in this school more musical than you, but what a waste! I can tell you this," and she looked at me in a curiously emphatic way, "the only way for you to become a pianist is to study alone and without a teacher. I say this not because you are so brilliant, but because you are so unteachable."

In those closing weeks of the year she imparted more pure information than in all the rest of the year combined, for many of my previous lessons had been devoted to tirades aimed at having some dubious effect on my nervous system.

"Be simple. It sounds easy, but simplicity is perhaps the most difficult thing of all. . . . For octaves, pretend you are playing only with your thumb. Set your hand in position and let the little finger come along for the ride. . . . Don't anticipate changes in dynamics or tempo; it's like an actor reaching for the phone before it rings. . . . To make this passage easier, place an impediment before yourself. Practice it with an extremely difficult fingering. Then when you return to the proper fingering you will be amazed at how easily it goes. . . . To make a rapid passage easier, imagine to yourself that you are playing at a slow tempo. . . ."

Joe had said, "Have a good last lesson!" and for my last lesson of the year, I brought Madame the Chopin *Scherzo in B-flat minor*. Half the pianists in school were coaching me by now, and it really went quite well. After working on it for a few minutes, she asked an auditor to leave the room, and turned to me.

"You know of course that you will not be coming back to school. No? Well, it is true. . . ." She went on, offering to write to Dr. Hanson for me and saying she was sure I would be welcome at Eastman or Juilliard. In her opinion, however, I would probably not make music a career. I was too interested in other things. The stage, for instance. And anyway, I was very nearly unteachable.

In the unlikely event I were to concentrate my activities enough to become a pianist, she felt it would be as the result of independent study on my part. Toward that end she had, for the last months, tried to give me some fundamentals to take with me.

"You are like a wild young stallion, Harry, and I am an old woman. To break you and saddle you would kill me."

Were these words actually being said? I had lived so long in mortal dread of this very scene that I could hardly believe it was happening. It seemed strangely anticlimactic. I had always imagined that such a scene would consist of a terrible lesson and a raging fury; instead Vengerova was speaking to me in the quietest and most civilized of tones. It seemed to me that a deaf man would have thought us merely exchanging the time of day, had he been there. It did not occur to me then that the deaf man would have seen my face, and that it might have carried a greater message than all our words.

At last I choked out one question, and as I did so I remember being curious at my own choice of words.

"Madame, does this thing have to be?"

It did. Without speaking, she compressed her lips and nodded her head in a quietly firm manner.

I got up and walked out of her room, never to return.

It was the end of the world.

UPBEAT DOWN UNDER

For the next three years, from my twentieth to twenty-third birthday, I tried to bridge the gap between that disastrous experience with Mme. Vengerova and the start of a happy career, with Allison as my marital and musical partner.

At first I was too humiliated to go home even for a visit with my family in Tennessee. Through the generous help of the school secretary at Curtis I obtained a job as a stagehand in the Philadelphia CBS television station (WCAU-TV), and interest in this job began to improve my morale somewhat. The station management became interested in Allison and me, and by the end of the summer we had been engaged to do a weekly television program as a two-piano team.

Encouraged by this success, and the financial independence it brought, Allison and I decided quietly that the time had come when we could be married. Her family voted strongly against our plans for a quick marriage, and we announced our engagement in September of 1948. Kit and Syd Wright gave Allison a lovely wedding, just as though she had been their own daughter. On New Year's Day, 1949, we were married at their home, Endsmeet Farm, just outside of Philadelphia.

During the next year I was promoted to a more responsible position at WCAU-TV and began to teach piano privately at St. Martha's House, a Philadelphia settlement school. Our television program, however, was a constant thorn in my side. It was a continual reminder that what I really wanted was to play the piano full time, yet my regular job was so demanding that I could do almost no practicing, and often played badly as a result.

The first people ever to take an interest in us solely because of our two-piano playing were John and Verona Slater. They liked our television program and, upon hearing that we had trouble

finding places to practice, invited us to use the two grand pianos
in their home on my days off. My debt to them cannot be measured,
for in those day-long practice sessions I began to find joy in music
again. Allison coached and encouraged me and soon I felt that I
must give up television and try once again to make a pianist of
myself.

As though these resolutions had moved the gods in our favor,
Allison was then engaged by the Australian Broadcasting Commission for a tour of her homeland in early 1950. When Allison
left this country, I resigned from WCAU-TV. Mother scheduled
one of her homemade concert tours for me, and at the conclusion
of it I flew to Australia in the hopes that Allison and I would be
able to do some serious two-piano work down there.

Word had gotten back to America that Allison's Australian tour
was successful. I was glad, for my little tour at home had been
what we refer to dubiously as "good experience." I had played
eighteen recitals, made practically no money, and had worn myself
out physically. Worse yet, I was plagued with dreadful attacks of
stagefright and played badly enough that I knew much serious
practice would have to be done before I could be classed as a
professional.

Traveling halfway around the world, I hoped to buoy my uncertain spirits in the crest of Allison's wave of success. Instead I
was shocked to be met by a tense and restrained young wife who
told me at the first opportunity that she just didn't like music any
more and wanted to give it all up! I, who had hoped to find
reassurance for my doubts, was suddenly engulfed in her flood of
woe.

The loneliness of her tour had been more than she could bear.
We had used altogether too much of our money on phone calls
from America to Australia, but these seemed only to increase her
loneliness. She told me how she, the earliest of earlybirds, would
go to her hotel room and sit up reading she knew not what until
2:30 in the morning, simply because there was no one to say good
night to. She described her afternoons, sitting in lonely hotel rooms,
looking at the walls, watching the clock go round. Always she
seemed to be waiting through dreary eternities in strange lonely
places.

The strain of coming home as an adult artist to the scenes of her former triumphs as a child prodigy had made her jumpy and nervous. Ordinarily an infallible pianist, she began playing wrong notes. Trying to nap before playing, she would just lie there shaking under the covers. During performances she found herself uncontrollably nervous. Like me, she wondered what the next note was going to be. Like me, she was possessed by an obsession that her next phrase would be a hideous blunder. Like me, she feared that her mind was unreliable on stage.

Worst of all, there was no one to confide in. If local conditions were unsatisfactory, to whom could she complain without seeming an ungracious wretch? If a program disappointed her, to whom could she pour out her heart, without professional indiscretion? What artist would not prefer death by stoning to the dismal farce of standing backstage accepting endless congratulations after a program which has been a personal disappointment?

In one sweet sentence, she wanted to give up music, and have a home, a flower garden and some children instead.

But what were we to do? Were we to waste my $700 fare to Australia and go back to Philadelphia so soon, with our tails between our legs? If you lack courage, stubbornness will do just as well. Allison and I decided to stay in Australia, keep trying, and see what would happen.

One of the benefits of changing your environment is that strangers will often view you with more respect than those who know something about you.

In Australia, the mere fact that I came from afar served to raise my standing in the world. I was a curiosity. The press showed some interest in my activities. I seemed to be taken seriously as an American artist. Shortly after my arrival we auditioned for the Australian Broadcasting Commission and were engaged for a series of two-piano recitals over their coast-to-coast radio network.

While staying with Allison's parents in Adelaide, Australia's third largest city, we settled down to the intensive practice which was to give our two-piano playing its first touch of professional polish. For the first time in my life, all circumstances combined to make it easy for me to practice. Dissatisfaction with my playing in

America conquered my natural laziness. Often in the past I had shirked my solo practice on the foolish idea that no one would know but myself. Now, the presence of Allison and her quick enthusiasm made it easy for me to put in long hours of concentrated work every day.

We became deeply engrossed in the problems of two-piano playing.

There was the matter of cueing. How could we play precisely together, without obvious cues which would be distracting to our audiences? We decided that cues were to be reserved only for starting together; after that, all else must be accomplished by acute listening, each to the other. By dint of endless practice we were able to eliminate formal cues almost entirely: the activity of playing a note produces bodily motion which can be recognized as a cue. Through previous arrangement, one of us would watch the other closely for this motion, and our cue was accomplished.

Day after day we slaved to perfect our ensemble (the art of playing precisely together). Pianos are perhaps the most difficult of all major instruments to play together, for their strings are struck by hammers, and the sounds produced begin with a sharp, plosive quality. The minutest variation in attack is painfully obvious to a musical ear. Unlike the piano, stringed instruments, for instance, can change volume at any time; an uncertain string or wind player may solve his predicament by "sneaking in" quietly and switching to full volume after hearing his colleagues' entrance.

Not so the pianist. For the duo-pianist, there is no answer but the discipline of perfect precision.

The secret of good ensemble is in listening not so much to yourself, as to your partner. To eliminate any question of who was right and who wrong, we began practicing with a metronome. For countless hours we worked, playing a devilish trio with that wretched machine. How I grew to hate that little monster sitting up there, ticking away, never yielding at any moment! Since more elements are involved, it is more difficult to concentrate on two pianos and a metronome than it is on the pianos alone. When the metronome was finally turned off, we could hear one another with rare clarity. It was the old baseball trick of swinging two bats so that one alone would feel light.

The exactness of precision playing introduced us to another

problem: was rhythmic rigidity inherent in this precision? If so, it would be hostile to all musical instinct. How could one achieve the spontaneous flexibility of artistic performance while rattling along as precisely as two electric typewriters?

To answer this question, we analyzed every piece in search of an intimate understanding of how the melodic fabric was woven back and forth between our two instruments. It was more fun than working jigsaw puzzles! By pre-arrangement, we decided which of us was to play freely when, and at such times that performer would play with complete artistic abandon. During these phrases, the other partner would follow and sublimate himself, much as the accompanist does for a violinist or any other solo instrument. It was exciting work, and every hour was filled with new discoveries about the music. Here, I have the lead; at this precise moment, Allison takes it over and I follow; there, our parts are of equal importance, so we must predetermine and closely discipline all nuance.

Never before had I gone over scores so minutely.

The difficulties of creating a balanced sound between the two instruments loomed large before us. How can the duo-pianists cooperate so that the sound they produce represents a single conception and does not betray the fact that it comes from two different minds and two different pianos? Excepting important internal voices, one may always consider one's bottom and top notes as the most vital elements in a good tonal balance. For solo pianists, this problem is relatively simple: your lowest and highest fingers tend to sing out. But what of two pianos, where you are one moment playing inconsequential inner voices, and where the next you play an inner voice with your left hand and a prominent melody in your right? Where your left hand soon strikes one isolated note which must fit perfectly into a melodic line your partner is playing in his bass?

Back to the scores we went again, analyzing every note for its relative importance in the balance between our two instruments. If this was what Vengerova meant by teaching myself, she was right; I was working harder on the piano than ever before, and enjoying it heartily. After ten hours of pianistic slavery, I would get up from the bench exhausted but happy.

Gradually things began to make sense. The discipline of ensemble playing tended to become automatic. Our minds were occupied with musical problems, while questions of mechanical precision began to solve themselves on some subconscious level, much as an automobile driver automatically co-ordinates steering wheel, accelerator, clutch and brakes in negotiating highway traffic, while his conscious mind is occupied by some matter which came up at the office.

The more problems we solved, however, the more we found. As soon as Allison and I solved the problems of cueing, we discovered the question of ensemble. With those mechanical considerations out of the way, we ran into the matter of esthetics: tonal balance and musical spontaneity. To say that we solved these problems is perhaps misleading, for they are never completely solved. Each is a musical ideal which can be pursued endlessly.

After those matters, we discovered questions of ethics. Could a conscientious artist, we asked, play transcriptions (works written for other instruments and later arranged for two pianos)?

Does this seem a foolish thing to worry our heads about, when there are atom bombs in the world? Not at all; an artist without sincerity and integrity is merely an entertainer, and while great artists are often entertaining, entertainers are seldom great artists. The matter of faithfulness to the composer's original intention is an important one to every serious performer.

Mme. Vengerova had used transcriptions, and Mr. Serkin had been death on them. Mozart, Bach, Beethoven and Brahms all made a great art of transcribing. After much soul-searching, we decided that transcriptions were acceptable so long as they were expertly written and in good taste.

On a suggestion from the ABC, I had agreed to arrange some Chopin pieces for two pianos. Immediately, I was filled with self-criminations. How could anyone find justification for playing piano works by Frederic Chopin in any form except that which he originally intended? Was I imagining him so stupid as not to know what he wanted? Was I setting up my imagination as superior to his? Was this not just imitating Grieg's talentless second-piano accompaniments to the divine Mozart sonatas?

Finally, I saw a possibility. The Chopin double-note études are all marked *legato*. This is often a physical impossibility, as in the octave étude, where thumbs alone do much passage-work. Great artists simply create an illusion of a *legato* in these places. Might not four hands be justified here on purely musical grounds? I decided so. To my surprise, those arrangements by no means removed all technical difficulties; the étude in thirds (G-sharp minor) is one of the most troublesome works in our repertoire, because of ensemble difficulties. In spite of the success of these arrangements with the public, I still questioned their validity and avoided them for years. Only recently have we overcome our reticence about playing them in public.

On such grounds we fought our battles.

We discovered duets, and worked on many of them together. Few of these were written before the American Revolution because keyboards were so short, and ladies' skirts so wide, that two people could not get at one keyboard together. With Mozart, the duet literature came in a rush, and some of the greatest four-hand music is to be found in this form.

Allison and I pored through Mozart, Schubert and Brahms duets. Personally, I was intrigued by some of the hand-crossings used in Brahms' *Hungarian Dances,* which were originally written in duet form, and often played by Brahms and Clara Schumann. Allison and I always became so deliciously entangled with those hand-crossings that I have since entertained cheerful suspicions that Johannes wrote them that way deliberately. He liked Clara.

In mid-1951 we returned to the United States, just in time for my twenty-third birthday. We had enjoyed some professional success while abroad, had saved a little money, and had laid the technical foundations for a career as duo-pianists. It had taken three years, but I had finally made a transition from the shattered boy tossed aside by Vengerova to a happily married young man, hopeful of making a career with his wife and music.

Allison and I had discovered that when playing together we were no longer haunted by stagefright. Instead we drew confidence from one another, and enjoyed ourselves enormously. We came to feel that the only way for us to find happiness was to do our music-making together. Dear to my heart is the memory of that hot afternoon on a South Australian beach when we pledged ourselves to a musical partnership. We must have the courage of our convictions, we decided. No more half-duo, half-solo careers. No more long-distance phone calls, and no more lonely beds. "Let's try never to be apart again," pleaded Allison.

From that day until this, neither of us has ever sat down in public to play a solo recital.

I BRING ALLISON HOME

One of the less happy aspects of our cultural scene is the pessimism with which many professional musicians view music as a career.

I have known lawyers, doctors, and plumbers, all infected with the forgivable foolishness of wanting to force their children to follow in their professional footsteps. But no concert pianists. Why? What other profession begins earlier in life, or on such a note of high hopes and enthusiasm?

Perhaps the answer is that society is not organized to protect the artist. The mass media of radio, television, records, and our highly organized system of concert promotion, make it possible for a very few concert attractions to dominate the nation's serious music business. There are not many openings for newcomers, and the competition for them is so intense as to be prohibitive.

Certainly every professional field has disappointed and frustrated competitors. But for how many must one's training begin in knee pants? For how many must one's childhood be sacrificed to those endless hours of practice? For any other occupation, labor laws (or humane societies) would prohibit a nine-year-old child from putting in his days at such a hard apprenticeship: for musicians it is an accepted necessity. The concert stage, moreover, is an all-or-nothing gamble. If a young engineer falls just short of being one of the country's best, there are still many fine positions available; if a young musician falls just short of being a concert artist, he has just fallen. Thud. There is no second foothold.

Allison and I came back from Australia filled with a healthy respect for the hazards of building the career we both wanted so much. Before us lay a choice: We could go straight to Tennessee and try to build on Mother's little homemade concert management, or we could do what everyone else was doing and try to start our career in New York.

Our ambitious friends all followed the well-worn path to New York. At twenty-five or thirty years of age they could still be seen living off their families, pale from lack of sunshine, with exaggerated smiles or pinched frowns hovering about their faces. Complete dependence on their families forced them to avoid many of life's major functions. At thirty they could not seriously consider a sweetheart, much less marriage. If they did marry, children often came only as the result of a mistake. The artist needs love perhaps even more than his fellows, yet his position in society is so precarious that he is often unfitted for the material responsibilities which society attaches to that love. As a result, his emotional needs often find outlet in tawdry love affairs which are more an advertisement for unhappiness than romance.

Even our friends with promising concert careers seemed a poor advertisement for the life they led. When one visited them, he became conscious of an undercurrent of tension in the air. Could they stay in the game? Or would they follow the familiar big-management pattern, do the rounds for a few seasons and then drop out in favor of another eager unknown? The uncertainties of promoting a career amounted to an obsession.

Professional people such as lawyers, doctors and musicians spend thousands upon thousands of dollars, and many years of work, learning how to practice their profession once they have managed to obtain a client. Almost none of their schooling is directed at the problem of getting that client in the first place. They leave school with vast confidence, and only the haziest idea how to cultivate a business. Artists are no less intelligent than others, but their background is often short-changed in practical matters. Suddenly, without preparation, they are thrust into one of the most treacherous forms of salesmanship: the art of self-promotion.

Like sensitive women entering the business world, they cover their confusion with brassy self-assertion.

If it were not for the certain knowledge that underneath this self-assertion a sensitive and refined artist was fighting for his very existence, one would think these self-promoting musicians to be a laughable and conscienceless bunch of charlatans. Take, for instance, one of my dear friends, whom I know to be a good young artist, and whose pardon I do humbly beg. Shall we call him Joe Spizzicatto?

Joe can never write a letter without "casually" mentioning where he just played, what a tremendous success he was, and where he is just about to play (for the second time). Ask how his Town Hall recital went two years ago, and he still has the reviews in his pocket; they are not sensational, but he trots them out, or quotes them from memory, bearing down hard on all the significant phrases.

"*Unusual talent*," he harps, and "*well-filled house*." Everyone knows what it *means* to use such phrases in New York, and Joe hastens to outline the devastated amazement with which the provinces will read these incredible tributes to his genius and drawing power. Perhaps you may have imagined that Joe was just what he seemed: a talented but unknown and relatively inexperienced violinist. Joe (believe me: he is really a nice fellow) quickly sets you straight. There is almost nothing standing between him and the very top. Heifitz has the name, but is all technique. Milstein is hard, Elman a has-been, and Stern has not an iota of restraint or good taste. None of the upcoming violinists are really satisfying (he says) and one is awed to learn that Joe Spizzicatto must be inevitably recognized at any moment as the great new violinist of our time. He has the fiery technique, the soulful musicianship, and the exciting showmanship.

Joe was always a fantastic success in the last town, though tonight (he admits) the audience is a little dull. With a knowing wink, he lets you in on the secrets of his tremendous audience appeal. "It's showmanship," he whispers. "Use your bow. Give 'em something to watch. It's nothing really," he smiles, "just tricks of the trade, that's all. Tricks of the trade."

After a typical Spizzicatto brainwashing, I was at a Curtis reunion party with Aaron Rosand, a violinist who went to school with Allison and me, and whose judgment I have always respected highly. "Aaron," I asked warily, "ever hear of Joe Spizzicatto?"

"Oh, yeah," answered Aaron, "isn't he the fellow that played that funny Town Hall recital a few years ago? Waved his bow around a lot. I remember he scraped it on the floor at the bottom of an *arpeggio* and damn near knocked out an overhead spot with it when he reached the top!"

Teddy Lettvin laughed from across the room, "Sounds like he's been playing in too many small towns."

Some artists have themselves paged in the midst of musical gatherings. Some drop names. To them, Mr. Ormandy is always "Gene"; Mr. Serkin, "Rudi"; and Szell is identified only as "George."

Psychiatrists tell us that fifty per cent of all the talking we do is to convince ourselves, and other people, of our own superiority. Perhaps this explains why good conversational listeners are so rare, and so much appreciated. We humans tend to measure our position in the race of life by what other people think of us and how they act toward us. When people cause us to feel that they think us important, by being attentive listeners, for instance, it greatly satisfies our deepest emotional longings; these people we like.

Artists are invariably sensitive people of quick intelligence, and should be the first to understand these homely principles of human nature. Unfortunately, environment sometimes makes them self-centered, and self-centered people are seldom able to lose sight of themselves long enough to encourage anyone else to feel important. It is too bad, for they could best further their own selfish ends by being genuinely interested in others. However unhappy the implied overtones, it is corking good fun to see a couple of would-be artists vying for the upper hand, like two old-time vaudeville hams.

One: "How've you been getting along?"

The other: "Fine! Splendid. Couldn't be better. I'm not doing anything right now, of course, but that's because they've ["they" remain unidentified] been keeping me so busy I just had to have a little vacation! How about you? Do you have a manager yet?"

"A manager? I'll say not!" shouts number one emphatically. "I wouldn't do business with those bloodsuckers. I had offers from both big managements, but you should have heard me tell 'em off! I told them straight off that I wouldn't put up with all those ridiculous schedule jumps and layovers. And that I wouldn't stand for being fleeced with all those bills and expenses they keep sending their artists!"

"Wonderful!" exclaims his friend. "Did you hear how Isolde Gutblatz told off her manager [one of the Great White Fathers of concert management]? He tried to tell her what to do, what to say, and how low her dress should be cut. Isolde really cut him down. 'What are we selling, music or sex?' she asked. 'If it's sex, I can get more for it!' Of course they tore up her contract, but they know to respect her now!"

These two blushing violets never refer to any town by its proper name, lest they be thought provincial. They never "go" anywhere; they always "have to fly" to "L.A.," or "Philly," or "the Coast." And of course the Coast is never the Atlantic Coast. One mentions playing in Kansas City; immediately the other enumerates a ring of nearby towns where he has performed. If it is a town where both have played, they try to outdo one another in casual recollections about the place, or in descriptions of the warm relationships they enjoyed with their sponsors there.

These pretensions are what artists are great in spite of. They are contrary to all our natures, and yet quite possible for each of us. Allison and I decided that a life which fostered such an insecure personality was destructive to happiness. After all, when I am with another artist, I am not in the least interested in a recital of where he has been, et cetera. All I care about is him personally (and a chance to tell him where I have been!).

If we tried to build a career the same way everyone else was doing, we wondered if we could hope for any more happiness than they seemed to be finding. Surely, we thought, there must be a better answer than following everyone else to New York.

Arming ourselves to think independently, we gathered statistics: America has about 300 concert artists who may be considered successful. Our society should support many more. Other musical statistics are like income tax deductions: one's guesses never approach the real total. This country boasts 150 musical periodicals, 958 orchestras, and 20 million music students! Even this is not the full picture. Those music students are constantly being graduated at the top and replaced at the bottom. Today there is hardly a person in the country who has not been exposed to some kind of musical instruction. As a result, thirty million people in America are genuinely interested in serious music of the last three centuries. One would not suspect their number or enthusiasm, for these people are sophisticated, and therefore express themselves less violently than the uninhibited lovers of what is called "popular" music. Noisy or not, they are there, and they should be a comfort to the aspiring performer.

There is perhaps one successful concert artist for every 100,000 people seriously interested in his field. Obviously, these artists must in some sense be leaders, and this is where many of our friends had failed in their bid for a concert career: they were hopeless followers. They had courage to do only what everyone else was doing. Vengerova had said one's art mirrored everything about him; could it be that this weakness was reflected in their music itself as well as in their careers?

It is simple to say, "be a leader," but how does one accomplish this? You can no more "be a leader" in general, than you can buy a railroad ticket in general. You must have concrete objectives; your ticket must be for a specific destination. The artistic congestion of New York indicated a vacuum of talent in the hinterlands. Should we not then commence a concert career from a Southern country town?

The argument that nothing could be done outside of New York was pure cant. Old-fashioned economics said that we could play for less money from Tennessee than we could from New York. We were closer to our clients, and it cost us less to live. What if no one else in the country was doing such a thing? There is a certain showmanship in flouting tradition; perhaps we would make people wonder what kind of serious music could come out of a hillbilly state.

Allison and I had the brash courage of all young things. We determined to play good music our audiences didn't enjoy, because we thought it was good for them. And we determined to go to the woods to take our business away from the established managers.

Knowing what I know today, I look back on that like a parent watching his first child falter across a hazard-filled room.

I wonder how we ever made it.

LITTLE BITSY

Most reputable managers estimate the costs of launching a concert career at between $25,000 and $50,000.

Allison and I got back from Australia with $2,200, which had been scraped up from every possible source and held together by the sternest frugality. Our expectations for the future consisted of a dozen widely scattered dates sold by Mother. They represented a gross of $1,750, much of which would be eaten up by expenses. With these skinny resources we planned to finance a nationwide sales promotion, buy two pianos, a truck to carry them in, and hold back enough money for operating expenses. It was not even a good shoestring; one concert grand piano alone may cost $9,000.

Arriving in Tennessee, we moved in with my parents to save money. Then we bought a used farm truck for $850, spent two barefooted days scrubbing the manure out of it, and got a country blacksmith to build a $150 body on it to protect our pianos. I showed one of my better characteristics in pestering all our friends for advice on the new (to me) problem of automotive transportation; perhaps I revealed one of my weak ones by believing only those who told me what I wanted most to hear. I was determined to be advised that the cheapest of everything would be satisfactory for us. I bought tires too light for our load, and they resulted in many expensive blowouts once we started touring. We bought a secondhand radio, and at the finale of every symphony, or just before the solution of every mystery, that obtuse device would give a soft cough and retreat into a stupid, dull hum; we grew to look on it as an avowed enemy, showering kicks, thumps, and other abuses on it in an effort to keep it awake. The country blacksmith who built our truck body was able to keep his price low by slapping on paint with a hand brush, rather than treating the galvanized metal and applying a special undercoating first. After we had been on the road for a while, little flecks of paint began scaling off the body.

Soon, all our free days were spent with a pot of touch-up paint, speckling green paint back into the countless bare spots where it was falling off. Unfortunately, our new paint never dried quite the same color as the old, and after six months' touring, "Little Bitsy" (Allison's pet name for the truck) looked as though she had a case of green smallpox.

I gritted my teeth every time we parted with a dollar. Not until we saw that my painful economies were causing expensive maintenance bills, while at the same time failing to give the service we had hoped for, did I recognize the truth of our friends' advice that "the best is cheapest in the long run."

Getting pianos was our next big problem. Allison and I visited the Baldwin Piano Company in Cincinnati with hopes of getting two matched instruments for a price we could afford to pay. On the strength of a letter of recommendation from Eugene Ormandy, and after hearing us play, they offered to help us get a start: They would give us a special price on two pianos, let us pay at our convenience, and charge no interest on our debt. Even with this help, we could afford only their smallest pianos. This was the first debt Allison or I had ever incurred, and even though it was for pianos necessary to our career, we hesitated long before signing the contract.

Wanting to help us all they could, the Baldwin technicians outdid themselves in preparing our instruments. To compensate for the small size, they chose a couple with brilliant tones and worked on them still more until they were matched identically in quality.

Unable to afford hotel rooms, we resolved that in warm weather we would sleep in the truck between our pianos. Wanting to accustom ourselves to this form of self-punishment, we made up a pallet in the truck one night and settled down for a trial sleep. A rain came up, poured through a hundred holes in our roof, and chased us into the house. The next afternoon (before we could patch the leaks) Baldwin called, to ask if we would pick up our pianos in Cincinnati on the following morning.

We had not yet bought any moving equipment or blankets to use for padding the pianos in transit, so Allison snatched quilts and blankets off every bed in the house, piled them into the truck, and away we went. This was the first of our many midnight drives, when whole nights were to be sacrificed in a frantic rush to get somewhere on a schedule. At four o'clock the next morning we stopped on a hillside outside of Cincinnati, made up our pallet in the back of the truck, and went to sleep.

Three hours later we woke up, slimy with sweat, and both complaining of wretched headaches. The early morning sun had heated Little Bitsy's metal body until it was like an oven, with no ventilation. We cleaned up in the rest room of a service station, changed clothes, and went straight to the Baldwin factory.

Our pianos were what are popularly called "baby grands," but we were overjoyed with them. How beautiful they sounded, and how thrilled we were to own and play on instruments of our very own for the first time in our lives!

On the way home, we stopped to visit a friend in Lexington, Kentucky. Suddenly Allison pointed at the sky: "It's raining!" Large drops were beginning to fall, and we knew that Little Bitsy's body would leak like a sieve! Hardly stopping to say good-bye, we dashed for the truck and raced toward Tennessee. As long as there was light we could see threatening storm clouds just behind us.

At one a.m. we got to Paris, parked the truck under a shelter, and fell into bed. We were exhausted. I was an inexperienced driver, and Allison had been watching the road as closely as I to keep me from killing us both. After this drive, as after all the others which were to come, we told ourselves that "in the future we must plan things so there will be no more of these midnight marathons." We did not yet realize we were in a business where tomorrow is always many miles away.

Next morning we moved the pianos into our house. Mr. Kemp, our local mover, showed up with fourteen men, none of whom knew much more about loading pianos than I did. Like a bunch of African savages working themselves up to a frenzy before going into battle, we stood around jabbering and building up nerve.

Finally becoming excited enough for action, everyone began to shout at once, including even the crowd of neighborhood boys who gathered on the scene. Hands were laid on the pianos. There were three times too many men, all were trying to show needful activity, and the confusion was terrible. Mr. Fortune, our piano tuner, was saying, "No, look here, that's not right. Why don't you . . ." Allison: "Be careful, be careful, be careful . . ." The crew: "Watch out for that door facing! Somebody grab aholt! I'm about to drop it! Pick up in front! Look where you're going!"

After two hours of shouting and near-catastrophes the pianos were in place. "If it's going to be like this every time," moaned Allison, "we'll never make it. We can't possibly go through this every day." Morosely, I suspected she was right. Today, when I see local sponsors watching our crisp, matter-of-fact loading operation with an ecstasy of fear written on their faces, I feel great sympathy for the boy and girl so afraid that their own new pianos were to be smashed before their eyes.

Allison and I had been sleeping in twin beds. Rather than be separated from our loved pianos at any time, we moved one bed out, and squeezed the two instruments into our bedroom instead of in the large living room. For the rest of that blazing summer we slept on one single bed (39 inches wide) so that we might reach out in the night to touch the first pianos we had ever owned. Mother announced disgustedly that in such hot weather she would not sleep with anybody in that narrow a bed *for* a piano, let alone the ephemeral pleasure of *touching* one.

She was neither as young, nor as romantic, as we.

Dad was announcing that he expected our bookings to pick up as soon as we returned from Australia. But, I thought, how? What could I do that he and Mother had not been doing? Knowing nothing about the concert business, we spent night after night dreaming up new ideas for promoting concerts. No idea was too wild for serious consideration; indeed, many which at first seemed most ridiculous later proved most successful.

Personal contact is a most persuasive salesman. Dad suggested that before our summer recitals we do a public relations tour over the eastern half of the country. We had no money for such a tour; a mailing campaign, the truck and the pianos had left us $1,850 in debt. With memories of our depression days still haunting me, I had a violently emotional objection to any more debt. Overriding my resistance, Dad lent me enough money to get on the road, and we set out to make ourselves known over the countryside.

The summer and we were young together. After the parched hillsides of South Australia, we reveled in the greenness of America, and the smell of crops and new-mown grass. I remember the pride with which I pointed out Americana to my foreign bride, and how I took advantage of her complete ignorance of this country to pretend greater knowledge than I actually had. When she asked "Why?" I always had a reason, right or not. We stopped by the roadside to admire meadowlarks and bluebirds, which she had never seen before.

"But that's not a bluebird," she cried, thinking of Maeterlinck. "He's red in front!"

One morning I stopped to show Allison her first mockingbird, singing on the chimney of an old country house. For some time we stood, lost in wonder, as that remarkable bird performed, leaping straight up into the air and somersaulting down again, never once pausing in his rapture of song.

We tried to learn the lore of the highway. "Eat at the truck stops," advised some well-wishing cretin. "Wherever the truckers eat, you *know* it'll be good!" We ate at "Truck Stop" signs, poisoning ourselves, and nearly going broke. We bought a directory of eating places, issued by Duncan Hines, and were disgusted to discover that he listed places because the food was good, and not because the prices were cheap. Finally, we settled on the plan of driving all the way through a town to choose a restaurant before stopping for meals. We always avoided the restaurants with large signs and plate glass windows, choosing instead the rundown but respectable place just down the street, where prices would be lowest. These were the places which never understood that it was the cheese, not the lettuce, which was supposed to be old. Still, we got fed.

The days were exhausting. At night we would shift the legs of our pianos into the truck's cab, making room for a pallet between the two instruments, which lay on their sides, one on each side of the truck. The space was so narrow that our 39-inch mattress could not lie flat, and curled up on one side against the belly of a piano. The nights were a miserable tangle of arms and legs, unsuccessful efforts to turn over, and cracking funny bones against piano braces. Each morning we woke up with headaches, in a stifling oven, as the sun bore down on our rude metal shelter.

At Greenville, Illinois, we were elated when an audition for Wilson La Due at the local college promptly sold our first concert. The money from this sale would almost pay for our whole trip, which removed our great fear of having spent money fruitlessly.

Each morning we marched into a restaurant, ordered breakfast, and took possession of the rest rooms. Once inside, I would strip, sponge off in the basin, shave, and put on clean underwear. Sometimes wash basins were not inside the rest room. As insurance against this eventuality, we always had our gas tank only half full in the mornings; if we couldn't clean up in the restaurant, we could always head for a filling station and hope for better luck.

In Fayette, Iowa, we sold another recital to Upper Iowa University for the following summer. It was very hard to have patience to wait that long to get our money. Miss Hotchkins, who hired us, left us alone in her apartment while she went out for an hour. The moment she left, we ran out to the truck, grabbed our washcloths and towels, and jumped under her shower. No schoolboy ever relished a stolen apple more than we did that stolen bath. I could never make up my mind whether we were more grateful to her for the contract, or for the chance to get clean again on that hot summer day.

The publishers of *Musical America* had taken a kind interest, and directed us to several regional booking houses to whom we might sell concerts. One of these was the Concert and Lecture Service of the University of Minnesota. Arriving in Minneapolis, Allison and I argued for twenty minutes over whether or not these people were important enough for us to spend $2.00 to wash Little Bitsy before going to audition at Northrop Auditorium. Finally, the truck was washed and gleaming in all its makeshift glory. Our audition went beautifully. We played on two fine concert grands, pausing every few minutes as David Simonds' voice came to us out of the darkness of the unlit hall. Afterwards he led us to his office, announcing that though he could not sign contracts until the coming fall, he would like to use us for the season beginning in fifteen months. Once again, it seemed a long time to wait for a paycheck, but we were getting used to the idea that concerts were booked far in advance.

If only we could hold out that long!

Like many others, Mr. Simonds took a friendly interest in our homemade concert management, offering invaluable suggestions and encouragement. Allison and I left Minneapolis overjoyed. This one contract would produce enough net income ($4,000) for us to live on for a year. In spite of the many fruitless calls we were making, our trip was proving a great success. My only misgiving was that I had spent $2.00 to wash the truck (Allison had been against this extravagance all along), for Mr. Simonds had never even bothered to look at our vehicle. We, of course, had expected it to stun him into submission. It never occurred to us that perhaps we were lucky he hadn't seen it. To us, that truck, with its galvanized iron sides nailed on a rough lumber frame, was the epitome of modern and glamorous equipment. Little Bitsy and the pianos were the first things Allison and I had ever owned, and we were vastly proud of them. In Tennessee we would often stand by our front window simply admiring the truck.

Teddy Lettvin, one of two (!) best men at our wedding, lived in Chicago. When we reached that city, his parents introduced us to Miss Dosha Dowdy, Chicago representative for the *Musical Courier* magazine. Dosha became another link in the chain of helpfulness from others which made a success of our little business.

She gave us professional advice and answered one of our most pressing problems by identifying colleges as the main market for our musical product. She also pointed out that we would soon kill Mother with the countless details of servicing our dates. Each booking required many letters to make the initial sale, and many more to set mutually agreeable dates, make hotel reservations, arrange for loading crews, and take care of publicity requirements, etc.

"For the amount of work it takes you to sell two or three concerts, you could persuade a regional agent to handle you; he, in turn, might book any number of engagements." We saw the logic in this. Once we had thought that booking ourselves would increase profits by eliminating commissions. Now we saw ourselves sinking so much time and money in the business of selling concerts that professional managers' commissions began to look reasonable indeed.

Dosha arranged auditions for us with every manager in Chicago. Three offered to book us, and gave us useful advice as well. Perhaps the advice was even more beneficial than the business they produced. Above all things, we needed to learn facts about the concert business.

"Keep your prices straight," admonished Clarence Cramer. "It's tempting to lower your price to get individual dates, and sometimes you have to do it; but word gets around, and if one client learns somebody else is getting you cheaper than he is, he can make bad trouble." He offered to book us if we would advance him a $1,000 retainer fee; we didn't have the $1,000, so that took care of that.

George Wildeman made a different point. "In doing business by mail, the prospective client has nothing to judge you by but the quality of whatever printed advertising you send him. If you send out sloppy printing, he'll expect your scales and arpeggios to be sloppy, too. Your printing must be representative of your artistic standards." (Once again I heard echoes of Mme. Vengerova's admonition to infuse my whole life with whatever I wanted people to hear in my music.) If one's professional brochure has imagination, taste and beauty, the prospective client will expect those qualities to be found in his playing as well.

Howard Will also offered to book us, and gave helpful advice about building musical careers. "A good salesman can book anybody once," he said, "but only a good artist goes back for the second time. Just check up on an artist's 'repeats' if you want to know how good he is, and whether he's going to last in the business."

We were beginning to get answers to some questions about the concert business which had always been sore points. It was costing us money to sell our own concerts, and we began to see that managers were worth their commissions. Also, the big-management pattern of running young artists through their circuits for two or three years, and then dropping them, seemed to be not a conspiracy to make artists' lives uncertain, but a simple matter of the individual artist's failing to be successful enough for his clients to ask for him back.

Whether we were dead from exhaustion or getting used to the hard comfort of sleep in the truck, we were not waking up so much during the nights any more. All day long we were soggy with fatigue. Sometimes we spread blankets under roadside trees and enjoyed a delicious afternoon nap which made up for the discomforts of our nights.

Money was so short that we began planning our public relations calls for late morning or afternoon: not close enough to meals to be obvious (we hoped), but still near enough that we were often invited to stay to eat. At the University of Indiana, Wilfred Bain, dean of the music school, took one look in the back of our truck and promptly ordered us to spend the night in his guest room. We pretended to resist, but, like the seduced woman of Balzac's story, we surrendered with all our strength. I was so glad to sleep in a real bed again that I could hardly go to sleep. The bed was so much softer than the floor of our truck, I kept waking up all night, unable to sleep in the midst of all that comfort. Mr. Bain bought no concerts, but he loaded us with a hearty breakfast the next morning, and sent us away with a debt of gratitude for all time.

Back in Chicago, Dosha Dowdy had told us to call on her friend Armand Coullet, a manager down in Jackson, Mississippi. Mr. Coullet was pleased by our audition. He would like to use us, he said, and four years later he did so. In the meantime, he gave more of the advice and encouragement we needed so much. One of his most helpful suggestions was that we sever relations with a small regional management for whom we did a little playing.

These people represented themselves as America's only nonprofit concert management, and their chief sales approach was that every professional manager in the business was dishonest. This in itself should have aroused our suspicions. They promised great numbers of concerts, and produced two, at $100 fees. When we got to town, the local sponsors told us they were paying $250 for us. We began to wonder just who was supposed to be "nonprofit." Mr. Coullet advised that it was better to be allied with no one rather than the wrong people, and we reluctantly fired our first managers. This seems simple to say now, but when we were fighting tooth and toenail for every dollar, it was difficult indeed to turn our backs on their loud promises of much future business.

We went through a lot that summer.

Our tour of recitals began. For the first time we heard the wayside garage man's sales talk: "You don't know how lucky you are that you stopped; ten more miles and this motor would've . . ." When the police found us sleeping by the roadside in North Georgia, they tried to throw us in jail for vagrancy. I could afford no summer tux, and played our summer dates in my heavy winter tails. At the colleges in Dahlonega, Georgia, and Auburn, Alabama, I nearly perished from the heat, and just yanked my coat off entirely during the second half. The audiences seemed amused by the brashness of my playing in shirt sleeves, but I regard the experience as good only because it taught me what *not* to do.

Some people have the erroneous idea that Allison's sense of "perfect pitch" solves the problems of piano tuning; this is not so. There are delicate mathematical relationships between each note in a scale. If a C major scale is tuned perfectly, the relationships do not work out properly when you begin another scale in the key of D. For this reason one must "temper" the scale, establishing compromise, or average, intervals between notes. C-sharp and D-flat are not the same note, though pianos have only one key for both notes. I remember how shocked I was to discover that a properly tuned piano was tuned out of tune. Not only that, but tuners do not need to have a musical ear. When two notes are out of tune, a distinct "beat" is heard, just as one hears a beat in the sound of two airplane motors which are out of phase. The airplane pilot tries to eliminate his beats entirely; the piano tuner counts his until he hears a certain number per second for each interval he is setting. It takes no more musical talent to do the one than the other.

Next, the young tuner must learn to "set" his strings, so they will not go out of tune the first time they are struck loudly. This is accomplished by tuning each note a little sharp (high) and striking the key heavily until the string settles to the desired pitch.

In the summer of 1951 we were still inexperienced tuners. At the college in Bloomsburg, Pennsylvania, we worked far into the night trying to tune our pianos. Unwilling to spend money for a professional tuner, unable to temper the scale ourselves, we worked desperately, while the pianos went from bad to worse. Around midnight, I had an idea, and dragged the college piano over, tuning each note of our pianos to each note on it (unisons are the easiest part of tuning). The pianos were a little ripe the next day, but we got away with it.

In Harrisburg, Pennsylvania, we went to hear William Warfield sing "Old Man River" in the movie *Showboat*. We were having lunch with Bill in Australia when he got a cable confirming $15,000 for eight weeks' work in this movie. Allison and I were so stimulated by the memory that we splurged on a cheap hotel room that night. Next morning our overloaded tires caught up with us for the first time, and we had two flat tires. All I remember is standing in the middle of Highway 14, crying, wringing my hands, and looking at a ruined $40 tire. The miserable nights, and skimpy meals I had eaten to save that amount of money all came sickeningly back to me. Our tour had its black moments.

In spite of these misadventures, we profited from Howard Will's advice about "repeat" business. Of the summer's nine concerts, a Catholic school in New Orleans, a concert association in Shelbyville, Tennessee, and the colleges in Cullowhee, North Carolina, and Bloomsburg, Pennsylvania, all booked two more concerts each at later dates.

At the Chautauqua Institution in New York, we were thrilled by an audience of 4,500 people. After our recital, Ralph McCallister, the program director, encouraged us with the announcement that he hoped we would become an annual institution at Chautauqua.

"Harry," he added, "your mother is not only a good manager, but she's the only gentleman in the booking business!"

After the summer tour, we took stock. We had played nine concerts for a total income of $1,175. Twelve new recitals had been booked, and we looked forward hopefully to the fall season.

At a late-night brainstorm session, we tried to draw some conclusions about salesmanship. "All things being equal," said Dad, "people tend to hire the professional man they know personally. This explains some of the success of your personal contacts on the road."

"On the other hand," I countered, "familiarity breeds contempt. Most of our auditions on the road were failures, except those for professional managers accustomed to buying from auditions. The average local sponsor never buys this way, isn't qualified to, and is inclined to discount anyone who comes to him on those terms. I vote we be more discriminating about playing auditions. Unless it's for a professional manager, we would usually do better just to make a cordial social call."

We noted that our pre-judgment of professional managers had been largely wrong; that their commissions were little enough compensation for what they did; and that they were generally far more helpful and honest to beginners than we had suspected. The one management whose honesty we still suspected had raised quite a stink when we severed connections. I proposed that we try to mend this situation in some way.

"No," vetoed Dad. "Remember the political maxim, 'Don't waste time on your enemies.' The political amateur always wastes his

time trying to convert the unconvertible. Make sure of your friends
first, and then convert the honestly undecided."

One thing that disturbed us during the summer was the blunt
way in which local sponsors recited all the wrongdoings of artists
who had preceded us to town. It was horrifying to hear people
dismiss artists we had known and loved all our lives with a quick
snort, "That jerk will never come here again!" We often knew the
artists in question to be attractive people, and yet they seemed not
to convey this quality to their clients. Some momentary petulance,
and they were ruined in a town forever.

They seemed to lack a knack for showmanship. Showmanship is
salesmanship applied to entertainment. It is the presentation of an
idea in a form which makes that idea thoroughly attractive, whether
it be a can of peas on television or a Mozart sonata on the concert
stage.

It seemed to us that we must consider ourselves as educational
entertainers. People have no wish to be improved, however, so we
must sugar-coat our educational pill. Local requests were so simple
that it seemed discourteous not to be co-operative; they wanted the
artist to smile, be gracious, and sometimes speak to the audience.
If he did none of these things, they said he was "cold." When a
professional refers to an artist's coldness or warmth, he means
something quite different; it took me some time to get used to this
difference in vocabulary.

Great artists, whose musical warmth and romanticism are un-
impeachable, were described as "cold" simply because they did
not smile. What is more, the local people *thought* they were making
a purely musical criticism, because they were unable to differentiate
between human and musical values. Mme. Vengerova had said,
"One's ears must first be seduced through one's eyes," and she was
right. It was tragic to hear great artists being dismissed as cold
simply because they were (commendably, I think) without artifice.
We saw that all our musical warmth would avail us nothing if it
could not be communicated to an unsophisticated audience. Perhaps later in our career, playing for more experienced audiences,
we would find no such problem, but now we were often dealing
with clients whose musical experience was severely limited.

Nothing disarms like humor, and I tried to make audiences laugh
occasionally to relieve the unsophisticated of their apprehensions

about serious music. At first I thought that just any laugh would be successful, and, in a sense, it was. However, there was much to learn. Milton Berle was popular at the time and after a good laugh I would often prolong it indefinitely by mimicking his, "Thank you, Mother."

In time I saw that such laughs were expensive, and tended to cost us respect. I still enjoy humor, but it can be a dangerous toy on the stage.

Smiling, being cordial, and speaking to the audience were easy, for they required no compromise in the actual music we played, and musical integrity was all-important to us. Much more ticklish was the problem of clients wanting music they had heard before. In New York City, much music has been heard, and that problem wouldn't amount to much; in Wetumpka, Alabama, musical experience is more limited, and a program including works familiar to Wetumpka could easily be trite and hackneyed. It is up to the artist to design a program which satisfies the audience's requirements while living up to his own standards. As an experiment, we worked out such a program and sent a mail-out announcing it to all the colleges in the country. The reaction was immediate and favorable.

A real boost came when the Alkahest Celebrity Bureau (sounds like a cold cure) of Atlanta wrote saying they had seen one of our advertisements. They were the oldest concert management in the country; would we consider doing business with them? We were not hard to persuade.

Going to Atlanta, we met Ralph Bridges and his cousin, Pat Rudolph, who ran the bureau, and arranged to let them handle our affairs in ten Southeastern states.

Ralph's father, Russell Bridges, who had started the bureau back in 1896, still took an active interest in its operation. With a bald head, proud nose, and succession of chins, he resembled nothing so much as a turkey gobbler, intent on stealing our hearts away. In his day, he had handled almost every attraction in the business, and he spent an entire luncheon reciting yarns about artists whose names left us bug-eyed with excitement. Perhaps that was the idea.

Nelson and Neal prepared for their first winter tour. In sweltering weather, we wore only underwear during our daily practice.

Allison made all her own evening dresses. Salvaging scraps of cloth found about the house, she was able to make one gown for $0.80. One of the most successful gowns she ever wore cost only $2.00. Everywhere, people commented admiringly on it. Often they wondered what it cost; at such times we tried to look very wise and vague, saying, "Oh, you might be surprised!" Indeed they would have been. Mother helped design and make these dresses, and we often thought of including a credit on our programs, like our more ritzy friends: "Gowns by Ellen of Paris."

Trying to economize, I designed a large mailing piece which I hoped would do double service as a selling brochure and a poster as well. As a result, it did neither very well. We came to call it the Big Blue Monster. Gritting our teeth again, we borrowed another $500 to cover printing and mailing expenses on it. Each sheet cost us a dime, and I could not bear to waste a single one. For days on end we sat around a table stuffing those junior-grade monstrosities into envelopes. Whenever one appeared with a printer's blemish on it, I groaned, unwilling to throw it away, and addressed it to some smaller organization.

For the first time in my life, all my thoughts and energies were being devoted to the piano and to concerts. It was becoming an obsession, just as acting, and television, and checkers and cards had been. I could think of nothing else. I was impatient with conversations foreign to the subject. Every day, hoping for new inquiries, I met the postman a half block from the house.

Our October tour fell within a triangle anchored at colleges in Troy, Alabama, Kingston, Rhode Island, and Shawnee, Oklahoma. It consisted of a dozen dates, and when we got back to Tennessee, eighteen more new ones had come in.

After the summer's experimentation, we settled down to a serious baptism of concert-touring. At Lincoln Memorial University our violent attacks of stagefright were made up for by hearing an audience cheer for us in its enthusiasm; we were engaged again. At Troy, Alabama, where two freight trains mated underneath our hotel window all night, we were engaged again. At Fort Valley, Georgia, our sponsors seemed to think there was nothing unusual in the half-dozen dogs in the hall who growled, snapped, gnawed, scratched, and sometimes howled their approval of our recital; we were engaged again. For the Schumann Memorial Foundation in Rochester, New York, I was so preoccupied that I walked out on stage with my pants unzipped; we were not engaged again.

That October, we had several days in New York City. A friend sent us to see Mrs. Anna Molyneaux, of the National Music League, a nonprofit concert management devoted to giving America's young artists a start in the concert field; they had handled such artists as Carroll Glenn and Risë Stevens. Mrs. Molyneaux (known as "Mama" in the music business) was hearty in her approval of our home-made concert management. Later, she went out of her way to send us a concert in Front Royal, Virginia; at that moment, she announced that we were too far advanced professionally for her management, but she picked up the phone to see what could be done with New York's professional managers.

An hour later, Harlowe Dean, of the Civic Concert Service, was listening to us play at the Baldwin Piano Store. After we finished, he nodded approval and asked, "Are you satisfied with your playing?"

"Oh, no!" we chorused, shocked at the idea that an artist could ever be satisfied.

"Oh?" His eyebrows raised in surprise. "Well, perhaps that's healthy."

He made some flattering comments about our playing, Mama Molyneaux's interest in us, and asked if we were ready for major management. "Of course we could make you no guarantees, we would have to have an 'exclusive,' and you'd have to give up all this," he said, dismissing our present concert business. We were unwilling to give up our bird in the hand, but promised that when we were ready for a New York manager, he would have a chance at us. Four years later, he took us up on that promise.

In the meantime, he revolutionized our attitude toward big management. Instead of being a gang of racketeers sucking blood from helpless artists, we began to see that New York managers were just like any other business people. Some were good, some bad; most were like everybody else in the world: plain people trying to do the best they could. Mama Molyneaux was a down-to-earth grandma who would have been at home baking apple pie in anybody's kitchen. Instead of exploiting us ruthlessly, Harlowe Dean offered constant advice and encouragement, and sent us concerts on which he would accept no commission. We began to discover he was doing the same thing for other promising unknowns. Such a man was not consistent with the bull-session talk I had heard while in school.

A month later we returned to New York and auditioned for the regional managers who stage an annual conference there each Thanksgiving. Ralph Bridges and Pat Rudolph were there, and gave us much help by telling everyone good things about our work for them. When the smoke cleared away, we had made a clean sweep of every regional manager there; I understand it was the only time this has ever happened. For the 1952-53 season we were guaranteed tours by Alkahest in Atlanta, Pryor-Menz in Iowa, The University of Minnesota, The Virginia Orchestra Guild, and by Celebrity Artists of New York.

The 1951-52 season, sold by Mother and Alkahest, included sixty-six engagements at a gross of about $10,000. The 1952-53 season was to include 103 engagements booked by the various regional offices, at a gross of about $42,000. Administrative details completely swamped Mother, as Dosha Dowdy had predicted, and we arranged with Ralph Bridges for Alkahest to act as our personal management beginning Christmas, 1951. Our pianos were paid for and we were out of debt.

We were on our way, but as our condition improved, that of our little truck declined. Little Bitsy, with her light tires, weak springs and speckled paint, was on the way out.

In the fall of 1952 her death knell sounded. After scouting us in a particularly successful recital at Fort Benning, the concert association in Columbus, Georgia, had asked Community Concerts to supply us to them. We thought ourselves quite magnificent to have forced the biggest management in the business to come to us, and rode into town in our most lordly fashion. A group of high-school boys came out to unload our pianos. One of them swung open the door of our truck body, revealing the rough lumber framework within. He turned to his friends and uttered a chance remark which still smarts in memory, and which finished Little Bitsy forever. Today, I am proud of the word; then, it tumbled all our self-esteem and confidence down to the ground.

"Oh," he said condescendingly, "homemade."

MARRIED TO MUSIC

No sooner did we get those regional contracts in the fall of 1951 than Allison and I began looking for a home of our own.

The more we became conscious of the nomadic aspects of a concert career, the more important it became for us to be *from* somewhere. My roots all led back to Paris, Tennessee. The green hills, the eroded gulleys, and the swarm of country people who converged on the town each Saturday—they were all home to me.

At Haywood's Barber Shop I sat in the same seat, served by the same man who had given me my first haircut as an infant. Nothing seemed to have changed. A checker game was still going on in the back room. There was the old pot-bellied stove with its skinny smokestack snaking upwards, the same shoeshine man in his corner, and the same piles of hair on the floor. The guard cloth around my neck still tickled slightly. The sun continued to bake outside, there was still a ball game on the radio, and they were still flipping a coin to see who would pay for the Cokes.

We decided to live in Paris permanently and, while spending Christmas of 1951 with my parents, we learned that the old Barham house was for sale.

Mr. "Bud" Barham's home was built by slave labor over a period of four years, from 1854 to 1858, about thirty years after West Tennessee was opened up from Chickasaw Indian Territory. On the site of the old house there was an ancient spring, which had never been known to go dry. This dependable water supply dictated the location of the house, and earlier had caused the Chickasaws to use the spring as a camping site when hunting. A large sycamore flourishing over it became known as a council tree. Today that tree stands beside our house at the end of its life, a hoary hulk nearly fifteen feet in girth.

For some years the old manor house was owned by General J.

151

D. C. Atkins, of the Confederate Army. At various times he had
served as a representative to both the Confederate and United
States Congresses. In the back yard is a little old cherry tree which
testifies to a practice common in his day: after his last term in
Washington, General Atkins broke off a cherry switch to use on his
horseback journey to Tennessee, planting it in the lawn after his
arrival home, as a memento of the trip.

Allison and I fell in love with the house, its tall columns, shutters,
and two-acre lot. We began negotiations. In daytime, we haggled
over its price; at night, we waited until the lights were out all over
the great white house, and then sat on the curb across the street to
gaze at it and imagine it already ours.

We bought the house on Allison's birthday: April 22, 1952. There
was a general, high-sounding agreement to forgo Christmas and
birthday presents until the home was paid for. That was a better
idea than we knew. Three weeks later on May 12, my twenty-fourth
birthday, Allison did give me a present, the *Better Homes and
Gardens Handyman's Book*. This useful volume told how one might
prepare a building for painting by burning off badly cracked paint
with a blowtorch. I bought two blowtorches, hired a couple of
men, and headed for the house. Forty-five minutes later we had a
$5,000 fire on our hands. We were off to a flying start.

Having learned about blowtorches the hard way, I switched to
electric sanding machines. It took three and a half men (with me
as the doubtful member) ten weeks to grind the old paint off that
house. They charged only 75¢ an hour, but I never saw men go
slower. Our new neighbors nearly went crazy with the racket. The
sanding machines screamed, and one of the workmen yelled some
song about Jesus at the top of his voice from morning till night.

After exterior painting and fire repairs were completed we decided to do a thorough job by completely redecorating the interior.
It was a summer-long struggle.

The paperhangers were typical. We wanted plain-colored paper,
with no pattern, to simulate painted plaster; it would have to be
cut off neatly at the ceiling, with no patterned border to hide ragged ends. The very thought of such precision was more than our
paperhangers could stand. "But you can't do it that way . . . it
won't come out even . . . the border don't cost no more, you
know."

In desperation, we papered one room ourselves to prove that it could be done. I called Mr. Paper Hanger back and showed him how we wanted the rest of the house to look. "Well, that's a mighty fine-looking job." He beamed. "I'll get started tomorrow . . . What? Paper without a border? You can't do it that way." (I point at the ceiling.) "The border don't cost no more, you know."

We ended up papering the whole house ourselves, although I did hire a professional to help with ceilings and a few difficult walls. He was a cheery individual who tore paper carelessly, saying, "Never mind. I'll just dovetail this patch, and when it dries, you'll never be able to tell the difference!" When it dried, he was done and gone. It looks terrible.

The house was not completely furnished until 1954. In the meantime, my parents sold their home and moved in with us. Their furniture filled up some of the gaps, though not all. We didn't even have a stove in the kitchen. My mother is a wonderful woman, but she can't cook worth peanuts. Dad never helped the situation much. Somewhere he had read that a tactful person simply did not say, "This food is terrible." Instead, he should arouse one's desire to excel by some such remark as, "This meal isn't quite up to your usual standard." Therefore, regular as clockwork, every time Dad sat down at the table he said, "This meal isn't quite up to your usual standard." It was more than Mother could bear.

In self-defense, Dad finally sold our kitchen stove; for years we were the only family in town without a cookstove, eating practically all our meals at nearby restaurants. We did keep a hotplate for breakfasts, however, and these served to remind us that we had made the right decision about the stove.

That first summer was given over completely to our new home. Very little piano practice was done, though I like to imagine there was a happy growth in our playing nonetheless. In our mid-twenties, Allison and I had reached a point when we felt that certain fundamental human longings must either find expression, or be permanently suppressed.

Vengerova had said, "Your art is but a reflection of your soul," and I like to think that the act of making a home together gave our lives a fulfillment which was soon followed by the beginnings of an artistic refinement in both of us. There was an easy relaxation in our music as well as our personalities; we began to take certain tempi less hurriedly; I felt that our breaths at the end of phrases were sometimes more natural, and that we may have become more understanding about some matters of style and character. Then, as always, we observed that any new growth in our emotional or spiritual lives seemed to be reflected almost immediately in our work as artists.

But I did not feel very spiritual that Christmas in 1952. After seven months of intensive slaving on our beloved White Elephant, we were showing it off to Allison's sister Kathie and her new husband, Ben Spiegel, bassoonist in the Pittsburgh Symphony. They wandered through the great empty spaces of our house, not sure just what to say. Finally, Kathie said the worst possible thing: "Well," she strained for optimism, "it has possibilities. . . ."

At least I kept Allison from killing her.

Imagine, if you will, the suspense with which Allison and I await each spring.

A hundred recitals—three to six a week—from October through early May. The pattern for each of these concert days is almost identical: two or three hundred miles' driving (five to eight hours), unloading pianos (one hour), tuning them (thirty minutes to two hours), concert (two hours), and reloading pianos (one hour). In addition there is a late-night reception after almost every engagement, plus assorted eating, practice, dressing and resting. No wonder Heifitz said a concert artist should have the constitution of a horse.

During the 1952-53 season I learned about other patterns. Late in the winter, everyone we met began to seem mean and unhelpful. After several months of no sleep, we began applying to ourselves the remark Dad always makes after a short night's sleep, "At the office today, I'm going to remember: it's not *their* fault."

But don't lose heart, we told ourselves. Spring is on the way!

Gradually we were developing good judgment on the road, but good judgment is the result of experience; and "experience," as our old colored man used to say, "is almost always the result of *bad* judgment." We had a lot to learn. Fortunately, professionals everywhere seemed glad to advise us. From the Baldwin Piano Company: "Heat and cold alone won't hurt your pianos' tuning; it's the *change* of temperature that does it. If your instruments are cold, let them stand in a warm hall for two hours before tuning, or you may have to do it again!"

Cliff Menz, a regional manager in Iowa: "Don't make the beginner's mistake of thinking you're paid for just two hours on concert nights. An artist's performance begins with his first 'Hello' and doesn't end till he closes his hotel room door at night."

Franklyn Smith, our manager in New York: "Relax; don't try so hard. In a restaurant I heard somebody saying, 'They were terrific, but that Harry Neal talks too much!'"

Ralph Bridges, in Atlanta: "Never complain. Speaking brutally, people are interested in their troubles, not yours. Even if local people are at fault, they will remember, not that you were right, but that you were unpleasant. Anyway, most artists' complainings are a sign of subconscious insecurity, and people seem to sense it." I remember a friend at the ABC in Australia, telling me how Claudio Arrau was given an inferior piano for one performance there. Instead of the complaining uproar they expected, he simply shrugged, said, "I've played on worse," and gave a "glorious" recital. There are many such stories, and they all end alike: the uncomplaining artist always "played marvelously." Whether this is because good professionals seldom complain, or because nonprofessionals often confuse personal with musical values, the message for a young artist is clear.

This was the fall when a high-school student branded Little Bitsy as "homemade." That Christmas we traded her in on a small van-type truck originally intended for bread or milk delivery. The rear six feet of the vehicle contained our pianos and wardrobe; the front area featured a little couch which served as our bed at night. When it was too cold, we used hotels; at other times, we had seven blankets and each other. We still cleaned up in restaurants on the road.

My last gesture before starting out again in January was to paint a whimsical sign on the rear of our new truck: "You're behind Nelson and Neal, Australian-American Two-Piano Team. Wave As You Pass!" Not long after, we passed Little Bitsy on a street in Atlanta. Some farmer was running her into the ground; she was dirty, dented, and in bad repair. Evil days had indeed come upon our faithful little friend, and Allison surprised me by crying over it.

"I want to buy her back," sniffed my wife, "and put her out to pasture."

But hold on, whispered our hopes. Spring, and home, are on the way!

In Blair, Nebraska, we were the first concert on the first series the town ever had. A howling blizzard prevented all but a tiny handful of people from reaching the hall. Their concert association's president, Dr. Jipp (as provocative a name as that of our friend, Dr. Fee, in Denison, Iowa), was so downhearted at their poor beginning that we played a free recital for them a few days later. The association invited the entire town as our guests.

A restaurant sign in Hector, Minnesota, warned us not to light matches near the water, which contained some inflammable gas. For a short time after it left the tap, you could set fire to their water; a favorite schoolboy prank was to leave the faucets running, and aflame.

That year, as each year since, we fought through snow and mud and sleet and ice, all across the northern U.S.A. Every day, when looking up our next destination, my eyes would move longingly across the map to that last Pennsylvania town where the northern stretch of our tour broke off, to send us racing southwards down the highways toward spring, and home.

We were so excited, so eager for shirtsleeves and sunshine, that our drive south began immediately after the concert. By morning, we had reached the beautiful highways of Virginia; every hour was filled with wonder: cold, gray clouds soon lifted and dispersed, the winter's blanket of snow fretted down into little white patches clinging to hilltops or shady banks. All the way to Georgia we plunged; gradually the sun came out, and our winter clothing was discarded, piece by piece. We sent up a shout at each first: the first leaves, the first grass, the first flower.

At the end of this marathon, we gazed unbelievingly at a pile of winter clothing still lying where we had so joyfully thrown it on the floor behind us: heavy coats, scarves, gloves, caps and snowboots. Warmed in the sunshine streaming through our open windows, it seemed incredible that a few hours before we had been in the grips of winter. After another such marathon in another year, Carl Jacobs,

our contact at New Mexico A. & M.; examined my padded snowboots wonderingly.

"My children," he said, "have never seen shoes like this in all
their lives."

Soon after heading south in 1953, we got home for a few days in
April. The grounds were stirring with life; our rich bluegrass was
dotted with iris and buttercups; the peach and redbud trees were
in full blossom; about the house, our tall elm and walnut trees were
alive with that lacy greenness which precedes the full foliage of
summer. The house itself was no longer quite so empty; during the
winter our Philadelphia furniture had been moved to Tennessee,
and now our wedding bed and furniture were in place in our upstairs bedroom.

At this point our manager, Ralph Bridges, suggested that we give
a Town Hall recital in New York.

Earlier, we had avoided such a step. It would cost $1,500 (a dead
loss; few tickets are sold to these events) and I felt this was wasted
money unless one had already developed a managerial setup capable of exploiting the reviews—if they were any good.

Ralph seemed unworried about the reviews. Thus far, critical
response to us had been uniform. The *Minneapolis Star* felt we
were "a first-rate two-piano team." The *Richmond* (Virginia) *Times-
Dispatch* called our Chopin "flawless." "Euphony of the first order,"
declared the *Kansas City Times*, who described us as having "aris-
tocracy and sparkle plus control of balance and rubato." We "made
a hit," they said; our Brahms displayed "sovereign authority and
control."

We had never been panned, and once in a while somebody
would even get rashly poetical about us. In Columbus, Georgia
(where Little Bitsy got that "homemade" comment), Latimer Wat-
son wrote a long and gracious review which said, "When they sit
at their pianos, the Neals seem to be alone in their own music
room, loving life, each other, and their music. It is that feeling
that they give their audience. You knew you were hearing not only
mature but sensitive musicians. They played with delicacy and
grace, with fire and thunder, and always with beautiful musicianship and in perfect accord. For the sheer joy of music—for the lift

it gives you spiritually, we commend these two young artists—and hope that you may some day hear them."

However cordial these reviews, Ralph told us, Richmond and Kansas City are not New York. If we expected to graduate to a higher class of business (and fees) we needed the approval of our nation's first-line music critics. More and more, he said, concert buyers were balking at an increase in our fees, with the question, "Where are their New York reviews?"

"Go ahead. Give a Town Hall recital," he urged. "I'm not worried about the reviews."

He didn't need to be; they weren't going to review him. If our reviews were bad, it could finish our career. Word would quickly get around, and we would be harder to sell than banana seed in Alaska. In that case, Ralph need not worry; he could just get another two-piano team. But what about Allison and me? Still, I knew he was right. In this country it is almost unheard of for an artist to build an important career without good New York reviews. The time had come when we could no longer avoid this test. My worries over the New York recital were not confined just to what the critics would say about Nelson and Neal as a team. I was still terribly sensitive about the musical failures of my student days: what if the reviews were to single me out as an inadequate pianist? I broke out in perspiration whenever I thought of it.

Dad pointed out that a Town Hall recital would make us practice hard all summer, and that alone might make it worth our $1,500 investment. This prosaic thought steeled me somewhat, and we chose an early date for the recital (October 6); it marked our fifth anniversary as a team. Upon getting home in May, we threw ourselves into preparations with an enthusiasm and intensity unknown to me in my student days.

First we chose our program.

Choosing music for use on our tours had been a different problem, being governed largely by the fact that we knew many members of our audiences would be inexperienced musically. The necessity of pleasing them was constantly being pitted against our insistence that programs not be trite or hackneyed. Early in our career, we used to program the Mozart *Sonata in D major, K. 448* (his only two-piano sonata); inexperienced audiences found its length (twenty-five minutes) tiring. Finally, we stopped programing it except for more sophisticated audiences. As a rule of thumb, we tried to have about six or eight works on each program; fewer might suggest such long works they would scare the uninitiated, while more looked messy on the page.

To give variety to our programs, we enjoyed playing a four-hand work at one piano on each program. It seems to be currently fashionable to play these duets on two pianos; however we find them much more fun at one keyboard, as written. Particularly, we have enjoyed the Mozart sonatas for duet, the many fine Schubert works such as his *Fantasy in F minor, Opus 103,* and such charming suites as the *Children's Games,* by Bizet.

One of our problems was that people like to hear music they know. The two-piano literature is somewhat limited, and this leads to a temptation to play indiscriminate arrangements. These are often so florid as to lose sight of the composer's original intentions, and we are very careful about using them. Still many attractive and popular works can be found: few people know the Brahms *Hungarian Dances* and the Schubert *Marche Militaire* were written originally in four-hand form. Perhaps I should make clear that when I say we dislike arrangements, I am not referring to works arranged by the composer, for in these cases his original intentions are preserved intact. Such works as the Brahms *Variations on a theme by Haydn,* Debussy's *L'Après-midi d'un Faune* and Ravel's *La Valse,* we therefore consider original two-piano works. Indeed, the Brahms-Haydn *Variations* (our favorite composition) were first performed and published in the two-piano form, rather than the orchestral.

In New York we would have a musically experienced audience, and felt we could play whatever we happened to enjoy.

Ordinarily, programs are arranged more or less chronologically; that is, early composers such as Bach are played first, while modern works are placed at the end. In Australia, however, we had heard Gyorgy Sandor reverse the usual order by using the last Beethoven sonata, Opus 111, as his first half, saving all other works for after intermission. I was most interested to notice how much more 1 enjoyed the Beethoven at the beginning of a program when my ears were fresh, rather than at the end, when I was more tired. We

were planning some contemporary music for our program. Strange
new music requires more concentration than familiar pieces, and
we followed Sandor's example by reversing the usual order of
procedure. Our three contemporary works came in the first half:
Bernhard Heiden's *Sonata for piano four-hands,* George Roch-
berg's *Capriccio for Two Pianos* (dedicated to us), and Benjamin
Britten's *Introduction and Rondo alla Burlesca.* Each of the composers personally wrote our program notes for his music. After
intermission were to come Bach's *Little Fugue in G minor* (our
only transcription), Chopin's *Rondo, Opus 73,* and our old favorite,
the Brahms-Haydn *Variations.*

Our programing was unorthodox but, we felt, sound. What would
the New York critics think of it? They could say either that we
were courageous or that we were stupid. I could see a good case
being made for either point of view. It was not comforting.

All choices settled, we began to practice in earnest.

While I was in school in Birmingham, the Pittsburgh Symphony
had come to town. A group of my friends listened to a rehearsal;
they came back puzzled and disappointed, reporting that the
orchestra never played anything through. Fritz Reiner had conducted an intensive rehearsal on many small fragments of only
a few measures each. At the time, we were mystified; today I
understand that Reiner knew right where the trouble spots were
and refused to waste time on anything else.

The economic pressures of a large payroll force conductors to
practice scientific efficiency in their rehearsals. Sometimes individu-
als are less precise. Perhaps the greatest art in practice is that of
reducing trouble spots to their lowest common denominator; finding that one finger-crossing or leap which has started a chain reaction of trouble. One great principle of learning and practice is
to begin with the simple, working toward the complex; even a
bad amateur knows to practice with each hand alone before putting
them together.

In spite of this, some piano teams do all their practice together,
on the grounds that it enhances ensemble. I have heard too many
fine chamber musicians practicing their parts alone, and too many
conductors wishing their men would practice at home, to fall for
that point of view. Each player's difficulties arise in different places;
it is wasteful for one person to mark time with simple chords while

another slaves over technical knots. Allison and I did only thirty or forty per cent of our practice together, and that, in the words of Mme. Rosina Lhevinne,* was reserved, "mostly for ensemble purposes," rather than note learning or solving technical problems.

However much we may love one another, artistic integrity demands a ruthless frankness between Allison and me. Perhaps she has learned a little from me; certainly I have learned a lot from her.

"For Pete's sake," she cried, "keep your mouth shut while you play. It looks kind of simple." She doesn't waste time with high-sounding words, but Allison gets things said. As usual, she was right; there is nothing to destroy confidence in one's music as much as that mealymouthed look on the face of a performer.

"Slow practice is easy," she said, "but don't pussyfoot. Work hard every moment!" Warning me not to bump the last note of my phrases, she compared it to giving a sharp accent on the last word of a sentence. "Sounds silly, doesn't it? Don't wander aimlessly. Go to the end of your phrase with a purpose, but don't let yourself clench the last note with a bang once you get there. Your fingers may want to do it, but that's *pianistic*, not *musical* playing."

Although four hours of sensible practice are usually quite enough for the student, I was doing eleven hours' practice every day. The heat, though uncomfortable, was good for us—keeping our muscles relaxed and supple. (Dancers tell me they like warm-weather rehearsals for the same reason.) Each day had a precise schedule of breaks and rest periods designed to extend our concentration and endurance to the limit. Surprisingly, some of my warmest piano sounds came at night, when I was fatigued and concentrating least. I was reminded of Josef Hofmann, who told Mme. Vengerova he had learned the value of relaxation in just such late-night practice. Working incredible hours in preparation for an early tour, he practiced limply at night—sinking down into the keys—because he was too exhausted to "work hard." To his surprise, tone quality improved during these late sessions. From that time on he became an exponent of relaxation.

One of my greatest problems as a pianist was technical accuracy.

* The great Russian teacher of Van Cliburn, who won Moscow's first International Tchaikovsky Piano Competition. She and her husband, Josef Lhevinne, were perhaps the finest duo-pianists of all time.

At the outset, my technical training was poor, but we cannot go through life on such excuses, any more than a man can justify being a stinker today because his mother didn't love him forty years ago. There must be some dividing line, some point at which we assume personal responsibility for ourselves. Without this element of self-determination, we would only be spineless slaves of circumstance.

Naturally lazy and careless, I had been playing wrong notes all my life. Mme. Vengerova told me it was a matter of weak character ("All technique is in the mind"), and Allison said I just wasn't trying. They seemed justified by my behavior, which was unforgivably erratic. Though I could tell no difference in my efforts, I established a pattern of playing well for important dates, and poorly for minor ones. Dwight Anderson at the University of Louisville urged me to play every recital as though it were Town Hall; I told myself I was doing so, but this was only self-deception.

Perhaps it was also weak character which let me replace musicianship with pseudo-showmanship. I saw fine pianists lift their hands high above the keyboard and I did so, too. (Vengerova: "Why do my students always pick up the bad habits of great artists, and not their good ones?") Sensing the importance of personality in pleasing audiences, I began to be careless at the keyboard, while depending on personality to get us by.

In the summer of 1953 I realized the extent of this trend and determined that it must stop. Allison is an unusually accurate pianist, and with her help these dangerous habits were reversed. It was usually not so much a matter of muscular quickness, as of concentration: remembering always to have my hand in place before every note. Sometimes the corrections were ridiculously simple. I was missing slow repeated notes in the Mozart *Concerto in E-flat major, K. 365,* just because of raising my hand too high over the last ones. I must have imagined it looked quite grand, for I hated to give up this foolishness.

Allison urged me to develop a skill recommended by Horszowski. He once pointed out that with all the things pianists train, they overlook eyes as an aid, or "trick" of technique. Horowitz uses his eyes perhaps best of all pianists. When approaching a difficulty in accuracy, he plays the immediate notes by "feel," while his eyes rove ahead, anticipating the passage to come. One does not see Horowitz with a mournful look on his face, gazing off unto the hills from whence cometh so little help. He watches that keyboard. We found that the eyes could be used in other ways. If one must keep looking at his right hand, while having some difficulty of accuracy in the bass, let him visualize the left-hand notes on a register already under his eyes. The effect is startlingly like watching both hands at once.

I showed Allison a trick passed on to me by Jacob Lateiner: tensing the arm slightly while playing fast octaves. In spite of all Vengerova's insistence upon relaxation, she never forbade me to do this, and even complimented the result.

In return, Allison finally persuaded me to play my thumb on black notes, and sometimes to pass my thumb under the fifth finger in a scale passage.

"Who says you can't do these things?" she scoffed. "Those taboos are all just as stupid as the old-time players who forbade ever using thumbs on a keyboard instrument. Of course you don't want to let your thumb 'bump' a black note, but what did God give you ears for?"

The amateur begins his practice at the beginning of each composition. Upon striking a difficulty, he backs up, starts again, and continues on in the same manner. He supposes this to be systematic, but the practical result is that the first few pages of all his music are much better rehearsed than the end, causing a progressive disintegration in performance. To avoid this, an experienced player often practices his endings first, working backwards toward the beginning. This applies to everything: scales, *arpeggios,* movements, whole works, etc. By the summer of 1953, Allison and I noticed that we had been guilty of this same beginner's fault, though in a broader sense. Each day we had practiced music in the order in which it appeared on our recital programs. Absorbed in our efforts, we often dallied too long over the program's first half, and then either had to work hurriedly through the second, or were so fatigued that concentration (and quality of work) was poor. We realized this on tour, after noticing that our playing seemed less secure after intermission.

As a remedy, we began practicing all programs in reverse order.

When our winter tour came, we were delighted with the result; as each recital proceeded, we progressed on toward greater sureness and certainty. What a change it was! We were actually relieved to reach the last works on our program, in contrast to earlier tours when I had the distinct sensation of wading deeper and deeper into a bog of sound!

All summer we worked with a metronome for discipline, and without it for speed. (Singers vocalize higher when they don't see the accompanist's keyboard, while pianists play faster when they don't know just how fast they're going.) We stretched endurance by playing certain of the difficult Brahms-Haydn *Variations* over and over, up to the tempo. These *Variations* were a source of joy to us, for great music, well written, tends to lie well under the hands and to be easy (as well as rewarding) to learn and play. There are other advantages to good music. When a great composer writes a difficult passage, it usually has the decency to *sound* hard, too, so you have something for your trouble.

Abruptly, in mid-summer, we broke off our practice to do a brief tour. We kidded Ralph about sending us to Canada in the winter and Florida in the summer, but I was glad to get the grocery money.

Allison and I were unusually happy that summer.

In spite of all our apprehensions over the outcome of our New York recital, the great activity of preparing for it gave us a sense of deep satisfaction. An even deeper satisfaction came with the discovery that our first child was to arrive early in January.

Delighted though we were, the new baby would complicate our schedule enormously. Allison would be six months pregnant when we played in New York, and our fall tour was to last until eight weeks before the baby was due. For these engagements, Mother and Allison designed a dress which we dubbed "The Town Hall Guessing Game." It had a large hoop skirt; in the back there was a bustle which came around to the point where the baby took over. The effect was quite deceiving, and kept her from looking like an ant carrying a biscuit.

I wondered whether my child would be a son, and if so, whether he would be like me. Would he like carnivals, the way I always had?

Looking back to boyhood days, I can remember a side show carney who offered $5.00 to anyone able to tell how he made a mermaid appear in a small fishbowl. For some reason I waited until the next afternoon to come back and whisper to him that they used a concave mirror. He gave me 50¢ not to come back. I wasn't much of a businessman. I remember a "living head," perched subtly on a coffin-sized pedestal. As a little boy, I had watched a magician saw through a box containing his assistant; being quite small, my eyes were in line with the hammock in which she swung below the saw's blade. I squealed and pointed, and soon the whole audience was down on its knees, looking with me. Most of all, I like to remember the sharpshooter who extinguished candles at fifty feet: on the last bullet, his revolver failed to fire, but we all heard the gentle puff as that last candle went out, right on schedule.

I'm still in love with carnivals. In that summer of 1953 I went to one, gambled for the first time (sure that they couldn't outsmart *me*) and got taken in a shell game, like any other hick, for $5.00. In a sideshow, we won two ducks whom we named Ike and Estes, and who provided a large part of our entertainment for the rest of the summer. Ike was a splendid, insolent creature whose fraudulent swagger explained completely why phony doctors are called "quacks." Estes developed rickets, became crippled, quacked sadly, and moved about by means of a pitiful elbow-hobble.

There were other diversions. This was the summer when a country relative came into town to ask if we would play for him. His critical reaction was, "If my hands would move that fast, I could pick 500 pounds of cotton a day!" (General U. S. Grant after hearing Jenny Lind: "She must be a fine woman.") I think it was the summer when Allison went to see Greta Garbo in a rerun of *Camille*. After many declarations that she was not going to cry, she had to take all the back streets home so nobody could see her bawling. Other people had trouble with their eyes that summer, too. On the day when some lady wrestlers came to town, seven old men visited one doctor friend of ours to have their glasses fixed. That night he saw three of them on the front row.

Think of September.

Think of those first crisp days when little boys begin to sniffle, and quick eruptions of color break out on faraway hillsides. Think of that vague excitement in the air, when you begin to walk more quickly, and when old-timers remember tales of Indian summer for their grandchildren.

In music studios all across the land, concert artists begin to bear down. Some, in spite of their publicity releases, haven't practiced all summer, and these days are a flurry of activity as they warm up a couple of warhorses, something old, something new, and a few "tee-hee" pieces for encores. For many of the rest, this is the culmination of their summer's work.

Minute precision work never stops, of course, but by now most of the basic technical problems have been disposed of; the bad leaps, the awkward passage work, the difficult transitions—these are no longer main considerations. Now, they are consumed with reflections and self-criticism on form, balance, phrasing and tempi (and was their first conception really right?). They rehearse under simulated concert conditions. Upon making a slip or mistake, they continue on until able to pick up the music again (as practice for such a mishap in the concert hall), and then pause for a while. Later they begin as though it were another "first time."

Laymen often think concert artists' practice consists of nothing but these final rehearsals. They might as well think airplane manufacture consists of nothing but test flights. Still, test flights are exciting, and September is a month of vast excitement for the concert pianist.

These are the craftsmen, honing their tools.

On the large map over my desk, city after city springs to life, not just as a community, but as the home of distinguished artists: Los Angeles, Santa Fe, Houston, New Orleans, Chicago, Detroit, Philadelphia, New York, Brattleboro, Boston. Sometimes in September I think I can hear all those studios going at once. The mental effect is like standing outside a conservatory and hearing all the music spilling out of its windows. All the soaring, dramatic phrases sing out; that cumulation of vital moments is intensely exciting to me. Just before a symphony orchestra tunes up, there is a little period when the musicians take their places, and many of them practice the difficult passages, all the famous hard spots, from that evening's repertoire; it is an exciting hodge-podge of sound.

The September before our Town Hall recital was typical of all others: a welter of practice, clothes, truck repairs, speculations about our career, widely separated reflections on music and musicians, and careful self-criticism.

Criticism is difficult; self-criticism is much more so. Whoever has gotten far enough to criticize himself as sharply as his neighbor is an advanced musician. At best, critical perception is a delicate matter. Allison and I try to look, or listen, without prejudice. Then, relaxing, we permit reactions to rise to the surface of consciousness as bubbles do in water. Failure to be relaxed may cause the mind to "go blank"; I remember Mme. Vengerova ordering me to pick up one corner of a huge concert grand piano. "Try now to imagine the fragrance of a rose!" she demanded. It cannot be done, unless by someone stronger than I. Tension lowers an iron barrier between us and our more delicate mental processes.

There are many competent artisans. The great difficulty for a young artist is to achieve that little extra something which bridges the gap between competence and great art. A noted painter paused before his student's canvas, and added just three touches of color. "Now," he said, "this is a great painting."

"How marvelous," cried the pupil. "I am only three strokes away from being a great artist!"

"Oh, no," replied his master. "Your work was merely good. It was the three strokes which were great."

Very many talented people come quite close to artistic greatness, only to be stopped short for want of "that last little something." The most maddening thing is that they often have native instincts which, if properly expressed, would be truly great. A pianist whose playing seems cold and unfeeling may surprise you by singing with the warmest artistry; the physical act of playing thwarts his musical instincts. One's performing personality is an entity unto itself, lying midway between the aspirations of his soul and the limitations of his fingers or mind.

There are some familiar patterns in artistic development. When a young actor or musician becomes intellectually aware of the technical difficulties of his field, he may be seized by inhibitions, and do nothing interesting for fear of doing something wrong. Instead of being self-aware, he is now merely self-conscious. For child prodigies, this is a dangerous phase; sometimes, suddenly aware of the implications of what they've been doing during childhood, they are shocked into musical and technical inhibitions from which they never recover. Exit child prodigy.

It is difficult to get a student to relax his inhibitions just enough to become an artist. Instead, the usual pattern is to break out into a phase of adolescent exaggeration. Then, one gradually learns to apply controls, working backwards toward simplicity and good taste.

The fine line between exaggeration and good taste takes a lot of our September reflection. It is a constant tightrope for the performer. Art perceived at a distance must be projected with broad strokes which might seem exaggerations in a small room. Up close, a painting may seem an utterly senseless speckling of color; from a distance it is a priceless work of art. On stage, when the tragic heroine of *Mourning Becomes Electra* rubs her breasts, moaning, and writhes from the waist, the projected effect is grimly moving; let her try it in the movies, where you practically sit in her lap, and giggles spring up all over the house. On an opera stage the hero may poise a knife over his beloved's heart, and then wind up for a lengthy aria—while the girl friend lies there passively waiting for something to happen; discard the perspective of distance by filming this same opera close up and the effect is merely ludicrous. (My uncle would ask, "Why don't she git up and run?")

September is a month of trying to make music vivid without exaggeration, and simple without spinelessness. Against the necessity for vivid projections, for peaks and climaxes which really sound like something in a concert hall, one struggles for subtlety and simplicity. After studying a work intensively it is easy to lose perspective and make tasteless exaggerations without realizing it.

In September, Allison and I plead with each other, "Not so loud! Not so loud!" Every ensemble player suspects everyone else of playing too loud. Ben Spiegel (Allison's brother-in-law in the Pittsburgh Symphony) tells us that once, when Fritz Reiner continually insisted that he play a certain passage more softly, he finally quit playing altogether. "Good, Spiegel—good." The Maestro was satisfied, for imagination supplied the sound he thought he was hearing. Such stories abound in every ensemble group, and point to the psychological hazards of bringing forth the conceptions in one's mind.

These September rehearsals are filled with minor emergencies. We re-hash the old controversy: "Was Schumann's metronome defective (too slow)?" A rapid passage is refingered; it went well slowly, but was never sufficiently tested up to the tempo—a foolish mistake. We argue about whether the piano's percussive sound makes it necessary to take some tempi less slowly than an orchestra (with its sustained sound) would take the same music.

"Don't display all your resources; always have something in reserve," Dorsey Whittington once told me; we practice rapid passages until they go even faster than written. In performances, that extra reserve of speed makes the correct tempo seem easy indeed.

I have since felt that we overdid practice with the metronome in 1953, but it is a splendid means of discipline. Good musical effects must be attained without rhythmic distortion (singers, do you hear me?)—and we worked diligently with the metronome to cure my amateurish *ritards* at the end of every phrase. Work with a metronome gives splendid discipline to ensemble (playing notes exactly together). Some artists excuse ragged ensemble by calling it "individuality"; I feel this is just an excuse for a lack of attention to detail.

The real professional always has something in reserve; self-discipline leaves him ready to face any sudden emergency without loss of control. Anything can happen in life, and one never knows when this sudden control may be needed. Robert Harrison, concertmaster of a music festival in Brevard, North Carolina, heard the orchestra's young soloist suffer a memory failure during a performance of Tchaikovsky's violin concerto. Instantly he began playing the solo part himself, dropping out after the young girl regained her place and composure.

A most outstanding example of such discipline is found in the story Mr. Ormandy used to tell us about Szigeti. I have never checked its authenticity, perhaps because I enjoy believing it. Arriving in town too late for rehearsal, Szigeti was unworried, for he and Ormandy had often played all the major concerti together. Szigeti arrived at the Academy of Music while the orchestra was already on the air and took his place. Having been told they were to play the Beethoven concerto, he settled back, prepared for a long orchestral *tutti*. Imagine his horror when, instead of Beethoven, the orchestra began to play the Mendelssohn concerto. It could hardly have been a worse change, for this work begins with a violin solo after barely a measure's introduction from the orchestra. Crowded into that brief moment were surprise, the shock of realization, and a whole change of plans. Without the faintest hesitation or loss of composure, Szigeti's violin snapped to his shoulder and he began playing Mendelssohn as though he had spent weeks preparing for it. The character necessary for such a mental transition, under such great pressure, could be a blessing in all of life.

The greatest hazard against which Allison and I had to discipline ourselves was that of memory failure due to loss of composure. Earlier in our career, these failures were frequent, though we always covered them up pretty well. They came mostly from me and, like wrong notes, were mostly psychological. My memory slips usually occurred in smaller towns. Whenever we got to a big city, Allison always warned me that she was extremely nervous and in danger of forgetting herself. Would I please be ready to cover for her? Thus put on my mettle, I invariably went through these engagements without mishap. After a time, I suspected Allison of using this device deliberately, but she always denies it; perhaps she wants to use it again.

In preparation for our Town Hall recital, I worked hard at self-discipline, trying to master those memory failures due to stagefright. Controlled practice, constant performing and refusal to take my stagefright seriously finally let me feel easy before an audience. As a distinguished artist once told me, "Just look out there and see nothing but rows and rows of cabbages!" (It works.)

Fear of memory failure is perhaps the concert artist's biggest psychological stumbling block. There is a certain humor in this fact. Once, before Liszt's day, it required courage for a musician to play without notes. Today, every artist performs from memory, and now we applaud a performer's courage (if his name is big enough) when he plays *with* notes. The first time violist William Primrose played *Harold in Italy* with Toscanini, they were in Carnegie Hall; Primrose had no notes, and the Maestro always conducted without scores. The subtly changing *arpeggios* in this work are a famous memory hazard, and Primrose was suddenly stricken with terror: "What will I do if I forget? Where can I look up the notes?" Looking down, he saw a man following the score in a front row. Ordinarily this is disquieting to a nervous performer, for he realizes that any artistic slips will be even more exposed to such a person. This time, however, Primrose breathed a sigh of relief. "If I forget," he told himself, "I can always run down to the first row to look it up!" Surprisingly, this crutch removed his nervousness.

Rachmaninoff particularly detested those music-watchers. Called on to play his famous *Prelude in C-sharp minor* as an encore, he saw a young man produce the score to follow him. Irritated, Rachmaninoff waited until just before the end, and then began to improvise a *cadenza*. The young man, startled, thought he had lost his place in the music, and began turning pages back and forth trying to find himself. The more he rustled his music, the more wildly the pianist played. Finally Rachmaninoff finished and stalked off stage, grimly confident he had ruined one note-watcher's evening, at least!

Most of our thoughts that September were with the impending Town Hall recital. Knowing how often artists reveal themselves in their first phrase, we worked on the opening of our first work over and over again with a tape recorder; we wanted that first impression to be a good one.

Sometimes I wondered if the minuteness of our preparation was really getting us anywhere. Were we losing spontaneity and becoming musically musclebound? When Schubert went through Beethoven's notebooks and saw the agonized corrections, and corrections of corrections, it all seemed pointless; the first version looked as good as the last to him. On the other hand, Schubert himself was plagued with self-doubts. Feeling himself badly equipped technically, this great composer was preparing to take counterpoint lessons just before he died. Each of us must do the best he can. Sometimes overpreparation may have detracted from our work but, perhaps stubbornly, I have never regretted excessive preparation. Just the lack of it.

With September dies the summer. No matter how much practice we have to do at home, in summer we feel like kids let out of school. After months of icy highways, discouraging mechanical breakdowns, sleepless nights and drafty halls, there is no place in the world quite so beautiful as Paris, Tennessee, in May. After months of trying not to sound like an utter fool in front of our clients, it is very comforting to come back home, where there is no intellectual activity above the plane of "When do we eat?"

But when September gives way to October, and that snap gets in the air, I always yearn for the highways again.

"Ah, you're pregnant." David Libidins smiled. Eying Allison cheerfully, he pronounced a happy verdict: "You're looking lovely, my dear." Libidins' continental frankness seemed completely friendly and wholesome.

He was recital manager for Kenneth Allen, whom Ralph Bridges had asked to handle our New York debut. Ralph's choice was a wise one, for every detail was handled smoothly, though Libidins' secretary seemed distressed that we were wandering around so unconcernedly on the day of the recital. "Aren't you nervous?" she asked.

The only way we could keep from being scared to death was to treat this appearance exactly like any other. Over and over we told ourselves, "This is just Blue Earth, Minnesota." Unlike Blue Earth, we came to New York a few days early, partly because we were unsure of how Allison (in her sixth month) would react to travel, and partly to do several days' rehearsal on the two nine-foot Baldwins which we were to use at Town Hall. It was well that we did so. Having used five-foot instruments for the past two and a half years, we had almost forgotten the enormous, rich sound available on full-sized concert grands. In addition, the pianos' added length made us seem about three miles apart when they were placed, bows together, facing one another.

"You mean you haven't been down at the hall all day, trying out the acoustics?" we were asked.

"No. I went on stage and clapped my hands a couple of times to see if the hall was 'live,' but that was all. Besides, if an artist doesn't like the acoustics, what can he do about it? Rebuild the stage?" No, he just does the best he can under the circumstances, like a pianist who favors some note which suddenly goes out of tune in a concert. I always remembered something Sol Hurok once said: "There are no bad acoustics for good artists."

Ralph Bridges once said something valuable too, just as we signed our first managerial contract with him. "Don't think your manager is a cure-all for work. No matter how conscientious he may be, nobody is as interested in your business as you are." We didn't leave everything up to Mr. Libidins. Instead, I went to work myself, drumming up a crowd for our recital. One of the recital manager's main functions is to "paper the house" (give tickets away) so you will have some kind of a crowd. Allison and I had always enjoyed our best successes before intelligent musical audiences, and during the summer I wrote to every major artist in New York, asking if they or their friends would be our guests at the recital.

I was amused once by a pianist who told me he never went to other artists' recitals. "If they're worse than I, it's boring; if they're better than I, it's depressing!" In actual practice, however, artists are the most perceptive and understanding audience one could hope for. Writing to all the artists listed in *Musical America* I admitted frankly that we were unknowns and had no hope of "drawing" an audience. It was going to get mighty lonesome out on that stage, I said, if nobody showed up. Could they come, and if they couldn't, could they send some friends to our recital?

It was one of those brainstorms which worked. Libidins reported that his office was flooded with more requests for tickets than they had ever had before for an unknown's debut. Artists, their families and friends, kept our Tennessee mailbox full every day with letters of encouragement and good will. A pouring rain on concert night kept the house from filling up completely, but we had the audience we wanted.

Enter Adela Harris. Della was a perky, seventy-two-year-old pianist from Perth, Australia, who had always been one of our biggest fans. Hearing that Allison was pregnant, Della flew to this country to travel with us and look after her for the rest of our fall tour—which was to last until eight weeks before the baby was due.

On concert night, she marched backstage, to help Allison dress. The doorman tried to stop her but she shook a wet umbrella in his face, and told him, in crisp Australian language, to go jump in a billabong—she was *coming in*. Just after her arrival, I remember forcing myself to smile and stay relaxed, while thinking mournfully of Leschetizky's remark, "What should we listeners not have been forced to endure, had not a merciful Providence invented stage-fright?"

Abruptly, Della began to talk.

What a stream of gab she had! ". . . And speaking of temper, Siloti spoke to a roomful of pupils with such force that his false teeth flew out. And would you believe it—not one pupil of his had the courage to pick them up and hand them back to him. I wish I could get that excited. . . ."

We laughed politely and Della prattled busily on, about nothing in particular. ". . . Of course, not all concert artists make good teachers. Sometimes they do things so easily they can't understand a student's problems. I remember a story about Josef Lhevinne. A pupil asked him how to play a certain passage. Lhevinne sat down and tore through the music, snapping it off brilliantly at the end.

"'But how on earth can I ever play it like that?' asked the girl.

"Lhevinne looked doubtful. 'Well, I don't know—but that's the way *I* play it!'"

Della chuckled heartily, seeming not to notice my silence.

". . . And did you hear about the time the Lhevinnes were in Berlin? Simon Barere came rushing in and said, 'Josef, I have just finished listening to your record of the Schumann *Toccata,* on two sides. Have you heard my record on *one* side?'"

Della's yarns, though mildly amusing, did not interest Allison and me very much. We smiled politely and wished she would hush. It must have been six weeks later before we woke up to realize that her chatter, however pointless, had given our minds something to fasten on besides the approaching concert hour. She had picked up a few tricks during her seventy-two years.

From the stage, I noticed again that Town Hall, like most New York theaters, seemed rather small. Seating about 1,500, it is an ideal size for recitals. The huge auditorium of the hinterlands is often better suited to prizefights than to chamber music or two pianos.

It is curious what an intense experience recitals can be for a serious performer. I have known artists, weak from fever, to walk out and play extraordinary recitals, telling later that illness fell away from them like a mantle, returning only after they had left the stage. I have had headaches, stomach disturbances and bad coughing spells disappear completely while we were on stage, and return the moment our performance was over. The degree to which we are controlled by our subconscious is still a ripe field for study.

I remember very little about that Town Hall recital, except for a feeling of watchful concentration. This loss of memory often happens when we work most intently. Sometimes an individual recital is such a vivid experience that afterwards it becomes our only immediate past history, and what happened earlier in the day seems as elusive a memory as that of last week or last month. On tour, we often cannot even remember what town we came from that morning.

I do remember a quick flash of fear just after we opened that Town Hall program with Bernhard Heiden's *Sonata for piano four-hands*. At such times adrenalin flushes into the system, giving one's hands a deceptive feeling of quickness and strength. The pianist's great problem at this moment is not to lose control, not to speed up, not to hide behind unrehearsed pedalings, even though these temptations may beckon seductively.

During performance, some departures from the rehearsed pattern may add greatly to the beauty of one's playing. These departures, or inspirations of the moment, usually consist of little exaggerations of different elements in the rehearsed pattern: *Piano* becomes *pianissimo*, the peak of a phrase may be a little sharper than usual, or the climax more powerful. Fortunately, these exaggerations, if under artistic control, may (in a large hall) project one's musical meaning more effectively than the perhaps more restrained way he practiced in his studio. This of course is the matter I mentioned before, of painting in broader and more vivid strokes to project over a greater distance. It goes without saying that one's partner must be alert and responsive to such changes.

The performer, however, no matter how immersed in his work, must always withhold some objective awareness with which to evaluate these impulses toward change. Artistic inspiration, often springing from excitement, is permissible and even desirable; artistic alteration, based on nervousness, is as risky as making important decisions when you are unusually tired or disappointed. The line between excitement and nervousness, or inspiration and alteration, is a fine and dangerous one.

With that little burst of fear in the Heiden *Sonata*, my hands began to shake slightly. When nervous, the hands are easier to control while playing loudly; this was in a passage marked "*piano*," and I cautiously increased volume somewhat to get a better margin of control over my fingers. Poker-faced, Allison made that instantaneous adjustment which always gives me the feeling that she is aware of changes before I make them. This feeling, of course, is an illusion; she waited a few discreet moments before glancing up casually to see if my face betrayed any serious trouble.

Expecting her glance, I met it with a studiously casual look and a reassuring nod. Such nods, if incorporated into one's natural movements while playing, are quite imperceptible to the audience. At the time, I was not as confident as I wished to seem; one nervous partner was enough, and I did not want Allison to become worried about me.

Art is largely a matter of balance and proportion; changes in one place may necessitate changes in another. Thinking ahead, I anticipated a sudden *forte* coming up a few lines hence. If I went into it at my present dynamic level, the intended contrast would be emasculated unless the *forte* were played louder than written. Perhaps, I thought, this would be permissible, if there were a later *diminuendo* which might get us back to normal again. No suitable place existed; in fact, a line and a half later we were to *crescendo* into *fortissimo*. These contrasts would not come off unless Allison and I began more quietly at the start.

The thought required to work this out, though only a flitting and automatic mental process, steadied me somewhat, and I began to scale back my volume as quickly and imperceptibly as possible. Whether she had gone through the same mental processes, or was just responding to my lead, Allison molded her playing to mine so closely that I could detect no trace of two individual mentalities at work.

This was an artistic molehill. No, it was not even that. The dynamic changes involved were insignificant and not worth comment in themselves. This incident, on the second page of the first work we played, is the last thing I recall of our Town Hall recital. An alert and sensitive performance requires such absorbed concentration on so many details that this trancelike loss of memory is quite common for us.

We did not stay up for the reviews. There were no regrets about the program, and we slept like babies all night long.

Sometimes when terribly thirsty I enjoy the torture of looking at a glass of cold water for a while before drinking it. The morning after Town Hall, I did not go immediately for the early papers and their reviews. Instead, I installed Allison at a restaurant and had her order breakfast, while I went to a newsstand. I didn't even cheat by reading the reviews before getting back to her. Perhaps I should have carried it a bit farther, and waited until after breakfast before reading them at all.

With faint praise were we damned.

The first half of our program, as I have mentioned, had consisted of contemporary music. We were convinced that this music was worth playing. The *Times* and the *Herald-Tribune* went to some pains to suggest that we need not have bothered. About us personally, their remarks were dismal—worse than cruel—for both papers seemed to look kindly for something nice to say, and to have a hard time finding it.

"Able pianists," said the *Times*, but our work together was "not impressive." The *Herald-Tribune* accused us of "excellent teamwork," but concluded that we had "practically no excitement and dash."

I could not touch my breakfast. In five years of playing together, Allison and I had never once before received an unenthusiastic review. We had become spoiled. Now, for the most important and perhaps best prepared performance of our career, we had left these critics cold. Why? We had no idea how to take it.

We were filled with the most dreadful thoughts. What would Ralph and our other managers say? Would our concert business fail after this? Why on earth had we wasted our hard-earned $1,500 on a gamble such as these recitals must always be?

Some friends tried to comfort us by unleashing all the familiar attacks upon unfavorable critics: that they are ignorant, or like to play God, or only heard part of the program, or that their true function should be to encourage rather than to destroy. These beliefs are a convenient opiate for incompetents. It is inevitable that some critics should be ignorant, and that others make mistakes, but by and large, the professional critic is as sincere and competent at his work as any other craftsman. Much later, Dad pointed out that we learn more from the criticism of those who don't like us than from the approval of those who do. (Remember the Prussian military axiom: "It is a duty to learn from one's enemy.") Certainly Allison and I examined our playing in a new light after the disappointment of these two reviews, which so conspicuously agreed with one another.

Glumly, I called on Franklyn Smith and Jeannette Ferreira, our personal managers in New York. "What happened to you last night?" asked Franklyn.

"Nothing," I replied. "No excuses. We played as well as we play, and they just didn't like it. That was all."

"No," Franklyn insisted, "that was not all." We had been, he said, far more inhibited at Town Hall than when he had heard us perform on the road. "Artists," he said, "frequently tighten up so much when they get to New York that you hardly recognize their performance."

Jeannette confirmed his remarks, saying that when she worked for NCAC she heard Marian Anderson in New York several times before hearing her on the road away from the pressures of the big city. The transformation from a tense to a relaxed performance was amazing. It was as though she had never heard Marian Anderson sing before.

Perhaps, I thought, they were right—though I suspected there was more to it than that. It was true, Allison and I had been exceedingly cautious and careful the night before. Looking back over the summer, I wondered if too much of our preparation had been aimed at *avoiding mistakes;* this would have been a negative approach, and a preoccupation with mere correctness might have washed our playing clean of much which made it interesting. I thought about all that metronome practice, and my heart sank.

"Anyway," Franklyn tried to comfort me, "you can salvage some usable quotes out of the reviews. Everybody always does."

For the benefit of those readers not familiar with the concert business, it is customary for one's advertising to include brief quotes from various newspapers. Adroit editing and use of dots may get good quotes from the worst of reviews. "The most marvelous . . . Beethoven ever heard," a pianist's advertising might say. The three dots indicate deletion of "unnecessary" words; in this case: "The most marvelous butchery of Beethoven ever heard."

It happens every day.

I never have approved of this editing, for it circumvents the critic's real intention. This cannot be condoned any more than we approve of artists who tamper with the composer's intentions as stated in his music. (I feel this last holds true even though the artist may be Horowitz taking octaves in the bass where only single notes were indicated.) The moment Franklyn said we could always salvage something, I decided never to use any portion of either of those two reviews in our advertising. (It was a decision made under the influence of disappointment, but I was willing to stick to it.) The critics had clearly been unimpressed, and it would be dishonest for us ever to suggest otherwise. So.

Allison and I were so blue that we got a hotel room for the night instead of staying in our truck. Confidence shattered, I picked up the three evening papers and carried them to our room. Allison was in the bathroom, and I opened the *New York Post* quietly to keep her from knowing I had the reviews, which she dreaded fully as much as I.

On page 80 I found us, and began to read, apprehensively at first and then unbelievingly. Harriett Johnson's review was just what we had hoped for!

"The sprightly Australian-American piano duo of Nelson and Neal made it apparent last night in Town Hall that they have not been wool-gathering either in Australia or here since their joining up as a team five years ago. The pianists gave a vivifying impetus to the current musical season," she said. "The duo-pianists showed keen musical insight as well as a mellifluous approach to the keyboard. They performed with a relaxation which spelled intellectual and emotional rapport, together with joy in their job." Our playing, she announced, "was excellent."

"Whoopee!" I snapped open the *World-Telegram*.

Under the headline, *"Mr. 'n' Mrs. Pair Talent on 2 Pianos,"* Robert Bagar said, "These young pianists made an excellent pair of ensemble players. Their work always showed the quality of unanimity."

Heaven be praised, he joined the *Post* in liking our modern music! "Also, their best media were the modern items, all three of which got technically fine and—you might say—devotional attention." He spoke of our "absorbing delivery."

Allison was screaming at me to let her see those papers. Poking the first two reviews into the bathroom, I began shouting my way through Miles Kastendieck's column for the *Journal-American:*

"Providing novelty not only themselves but also in their program-making, they won immediate favor for the freshness and the quality of their performance." "Whoopee! Did you hear that, honey? Listen to this:"

"A fine sense of ensemble and accomplished pianism distin-guished their teamwork." (Bless you, Miles, bless you!) "What caught attention was their essentially musical playing as distinct from the mechanical, chromium-polished matter-of-factness all too common in two-piano work." (Oh, thank God!) "Their concern with contemporary music was noteworthy . . . these works all justified inclusion in the recital." (Take *that*, Mr. Morning Papers!) "Both played with technical security and accomplishment, awareness of tonal values, and keen musicianship."

His review concluded with a one-sentence paragraph which made the whole recital worth while to us and to our career. It was the simple observation, "They make a fine team."

Next morning, John Ortiz, Artist Manager for the Baldwin Piano Company, called us to his office and shoved a slip of paper under my nose. "Well, Mr. Neal—and your charming bride—" (he is not a Latin for nothing) "would you please sign this?"

"What is it?"

"It's a receipt for the two concert grand pianos you used last Tuesday night. The Baldwin Company is presenting you with these two beautifully matched instruments, for we feel you will be as much a credit to them as they will be to you."

Our cup ran over.

The $1,500 gamble which I was decrying only twenty-four hours before had run the gamut from a terrible disaster to the wildest success. (Fortunately the developments occurred in that order.) We had enough press material for our managers to swim in, and now we were the recipients of two glorious pianos worth ten times the cost of the recital.

As Della Harris, Allison and I pulled happily out of town, my little wife sat on the hood over our truck's motor (in the cab), clasped strong hands about her knees like a child, and smiled hap-pily.

"What kind of trouble are you about to get into?" I asked.

"Not just me—both of us," she replied.

"What do you mean?"

In answer, she began to quote from memory the last paragraph of Harriett Johnson's review in the *New York Post:*

"Pardon the digression. But a special mention for Allison Nelson Neal who, pianistically was first-rate, made a charming picture as well, and in addition appeared to be taking good care of a potential Neal who's starting his musical education in the prenatal stage. If exposure means anything, he should be a genius."

That didn't make Allison mad at all.

Women have a union.

They enjoy funerals and cry at weddings; they are marvelously agreeable before marriage and difficult afterwards; they hang ridiculous little towels in the bathroom and then chastise you for using them. By their very contrariness do these creatures rule us, and hold us in subjugation. Try to be mean, and they laugh at you; make them happy, and they cry; be gentle, and they say act like a man; act like a man, and you're a brute; turn out the lights, and they want to make love in the sunshine.

Their ways are mysterious and defy masculine comprehension.

One thing we men can understand: they stick together worse than doctors. Since time immemorial they have held the male sex in place with the best, and simplest, of points—we cannot bear children.

May I quote an aged female relation of mine? "You men think you suffer in wars. No matter what a man suffers, even though he be blown to bits and have his arms torn from their sockets, he'll never know what we women go through. A minute's pleasure for him, and we go through the tortures of the damned"—this last word being strung out over several running seconds. This charming lady never misses an opportunity to remind us of "poor Aunt Liza, who was in childbirth for *two whole days!*" Her husband tells me this tasty morsel has been served up at breakfast every other morning for forty years. Just imagine all the women who come backstage, gushing to Allison, "I was going to be a concert pianist, but I got married instead." Sometimes I look at their husbands and think of their helpless frustration during all those breakfast-table skirmishes: "Oh, I could have been a great artist, and had the world at my feet by now, if I hadn't married you!" This conveniently unanswerable logic reminds me of our Southern ladies who spent a lifetime blaming Yankee soldiers for the loss of family silver they never had in the first place.

The women do have a union, but my wife is a scab. A very pretty little scab, but that does not alter the fact.

She refused to abide by standard female working conditions. She had announced that cravings for food, and morning sickness were just psychological manifestations. Whether they are or not I have no idea, but after she became pregnant, the family settled down to watch her eat crow. We ate it ourselves when she showed none of these symptoms.

Allison studied books on birth and motherhood as thoroughly as though it were a new concerto and not a baby she was producing. Her doctor was shocked by the knowledge she accumulated on gory birth complications.

"Leave the books to me," he ordered.

She kept on reading and discovered that, contrary to tales we'd heard, travel should have no effect on her pregnancy. "How long can I play concerts?" she demanded.

Dr. Rhea grinned. "As long as you can get that close to the piano, I suppose." This was the point when Allison told Ralph Bridges to schedule recitals up until eight weeks before the baby was due. "I wouldn't take even that long a vacation," she teased, "but my arms are short!"

"When can I start playing again?" she asked.

"Not for a month, at least," cautioned Dr. Rhea.

At home she laughed, "Nonsense. If I were an Indian squaw, I'd deliver the baby myself and make supper afterwards." She had Ralph schedule our first recital (in Paris, Tennessee) for two weeks and two days after the baby's arrival, on January 12. Most of the women in town turned out for the concert just to see if she'd make it. Four days later we left on tour, laughing over a local lady who went to Allison's nurse asking if it was true what "they" were saying—that Australian women had babies easier than American.

"No," chuckled Brooksie. "It's just the same."

Do men ever feel more useless than at births and weddings? I tried to ask Allison if she was perhaps reckless. "I'm a strong, healthy animal," she answered, "and there's no reason why I can't drop my calf as easily as any cow does. The average woman doesn't hold the stage except at weddings and births, so she makes all the fuss possible then. Not me."

And she didn't. The first baby took twenty hours of labor, but she never uttered so much as a whimper in pain; instead, she lay quietly relaxed and let her body do its work. For our second baby, two years later, the nurse refused to believe Allison was in enough pain to require anesthetic, "because she's not red in the face or hollering any yet." After our third child, the nurses complained that she stayed so relaxed it was necessary to keep a hand on her stomach to tell when she was having a contraction.

I am very proud of my wife. Her self-enrichment, whether it be having babies, planting flowers, or painting houses, Allison passes on to others through her music. Who is a more lucky mate than I?

But I was unlucky in one thing. Everybody these days spends a lot of time preparing the expectant mother for the great experience before her; nobody prepared *me* for anything. All the babies I had ever seen were chubby little things at least three months old, and I had no reason to suspect that ours would be any different. When John Murray Neal (named for Allison's father and brother) arrived, he was wrinkled, red, without chin or forehead, and had a head shaped like an Eversharp pencil. For months the poor child was called "Bullet" (head) by our whole family.

Hard as we had tried to have a baby, as many tests and temperatures as we had taken, I still couldn't work up much enthusiasm over the final product. For me, there were no open-armed and exultant shouts of, "My baby!" Instead, I felt like an old hound, who bristles his neck and growls suspiciously at the sight of his new offspring.

Even Allison's iron confidence seemed shaken. To Mother and Dad: "He's not very pretty," she faltered, "but maybe he'll get better as time goes by." When alone they howled with laughter.

People came in and pronounced the child beautiful; I worried about their eyesight. People described his crying as "sweet"; I worried about their intelligence. People claimed that he resembled every known ancestor in our family; I worried about their honesty. After having three children, I can at last see that people like to admire new babies because they see potentialities—because they are remembering the happiness of other little babies—and not because this one is actually what they say it is.

"Naturally, you won't practice while the baby's asleep," warned our tiptoeing friends. The first day little John came home from the hospital, we put his basket between the pianos and started to work. He promptly went to sleep. I was not sure whether to be delighted or insulted. That Sunday, Myra Hess broadcast from Carnegie Hall with the New York Philharmonic. She was the first artist I'd ever heard in New York, and as a sentimental gesture we brought John in to let him hear her also. He went to sleep. I began to suspect he'd make out all right in our house.

"Babies are adjustable," we'd been told. This I knew was our only hope. Many elements in our life could not be changed without damage to our career. The problem was for us to adjust to him personally, and for the baby to adjust to us professionally.

Those of you who have been parents, consider our problem. It was our first child, and parenthood was a fearful, unknown quantity. All our lives we had been warned that children would end a concert career, or that by leaving our family at home we would fail as parents; we decided that if Clara Schumann could cart a family around the countryside back in her day, we could certainly do it now. But, we feared, a mistake of some kind might be tragic for both us and the child. We did not dare overlook any detail.

To begin with, little John must have a portable bed. I bought a laundry basket, which Allison prettied up as a bassinet. Dr. Rhea assured us that babies, like pianos, could stay quite cool; it was sudden changes from hot to cold which were dangerous. Good. If an Eskimo child lived in an igloo made of ice, John should do all right in our cold little truck. As a precaution against Canada's 20-below-zero weather, I bought some "pocket warmers" from a sporting-goods house; these could be slipped among John's blankets.

The child must eat. Allison was a veritable fountain, old-fashioned, and wanted to nurse the baby herself. This must often be done in public without offending our clients; we bought some attractive shawls and she practiced feeding John at home, while covering herself discreetly. We all stood around and watched, offering valuable suggestions. The mechanics of any esthetic operation should be unobtrusive; even under the shawl, Allison had to fuss awkwardly with her blouse, so Mother made two pleated blouses containing invisible slits, which allowed little John to get at dinner as quickly as he liked.

We anticipated that Allison could not always feed the baby—when on stage, for instance. How could we sterilize bottles on tour, and get boiled water for formula? I bought a covered pan, low enough to fit in a suitcase, and one of those electric heaters which men use to heat shaving water. The moment we walked into a hotel room, water was put on to boil.

Baby-sitters must be engaged, and I wrote ahead to each town, asking that one be engaged for us.

Most important was the question of whether the baby could live out of a suitcase. To find the answer, we divided his belongings into reserves, and those necessary for current use. The "current" gear was packed into a large suitcase at home, and in the house we let John live out of it just as though he were on the road. This two weeks' practice was most valuable. Every dirty diaper went in a plastic bag back in the suitcase. We organized our child's day around the hourly schedule we normally keep while on the road, and were convinced we could keep it up indefinitely.

This was the spring of our dust and snow storms, and of our midnight ride to Canada. This was also the spring when we often carried John into a restaurant and then got up to leave without him. How difficult it was to remember that we were parents—and how red our faces were when we came back for that little basket!

My father had never lifted a finger to help Mother with us children. That was not man's work. I determined to do otherwise.

Concerned for Allison's welfare on the road, I did every possible chore for her. The change to larger pianos after Town Hall had left the truck so cramped that we no longer slept in it, though our couch was still squeezed lengthwise across the front. We placed the baby basket on the floor and I insisted that Allison lie down to rest all the time I drove. I toted things for her, I helped her in and out, I moved pianos and drove, and changed diapers, and did most of that getting up in the middle of the night. Never was there such a husband as I. Solely through my thoughtfulness and consideration (I am really quite a fine fellow) Allison got through the spring tour rested and in good shape, though I was on the verge of collapse.

But nobody appreciated me. When we got to town, all the old ladies crowded about my sweet wife, exclaiming, "Oh, my dear, you look so lovely. How on earth do you manage it, with the baby and all?"

Allison, fresh and rested from having slept all during our morning drive, smiled modestly. "It's just a matter of good planning and budgeting your time," she replied. The ladies marveled. I—budgeted time and planning personified—they ignored. Exhausted, I hung over the steering wheel as limply as a piece of raw liver, and hoped for a crumb of sympathy.

"Don't be silly," they said. "Everybody knows the male has nothing to do with these things."

"WAVE AS YOU PASS!"

About a year later, I dragged myself out of a deep sleep just enough to uncover one eyeball. The other side of my face screwed up in a ferocious grimace which kept my left eye clamped shut against the early morning light, refusing to face facts. It was six o'clock in the morning, early May, 1955. Time to get up.

Heavily, I pulled upright. I was, to use a term overemployed in my youth, "frazzled out." There was sand in my eyes and cotton in my mouth.

Nothing was right. You couldn't tuck in the bedsheets on our couch and my feet had stuck through the covers, getting cold, all night. Did that account for those nightmares about unloading pianos in a flood, moving pianos up the sides of cliffs, having wrecks and being arrested, etc? After our recital the previous evening, we had been entertained at a reception which lasted until two in the morning. That was all right for the local folks, who did it only a few times a year, but for us it happened almost every night (twenty-two concerts in the twenty-nine days). What imbecile told me you could live indefinitely on four hours' sleep a night?

"Oh, Mr. Neal," people sometimes said, "I think it's wonderful how you can lie down and nap for fifteen minutes at any hour of the day!" Little did they know. I was usually just too tired to stay awake.

I had awakened with what Lee Dora, my childhood nurse, used to call "the mizries." How thoughtless it would be if I were to hoard this misery to myself alone. It must be shared! I grunted at a shapeless pile of blankets across the couch.

"Allison."

My reply was a sensuous motion by one leg as she snuggled down deeper in the covers. Silence. Then, "Mmmm?"

"Get up."

"Mmmm."

189

Silence.

Sourly, I looked about the truck. When John had grown too big for a bassinet we built a trailer for the pianos and converted the truck into fairly elaborate living quarters, along the lines of a house trailer. It would have been simpler, and cheaper, to buy a house trailer, but the law doesn't permit you to stay in one while it is in motion. Much of our time is spent on the highway, and I wanted Allison and the baby to be comfortable during those long hours.

In my optimistic moods this rig was an ingenious answer to the problems of concert touring. In black moods (right then, for instance) it was hell on four wheels.

In the first place, nobody knew what to call it. The truck was outfitted like a house trailer. If I spoke of the trailer (meaning the trailer), everyone thought I meant the truck. If they mentioned the trailer (meaning the truck), I thought they meant the trailer. Nuts.

That trailer had enjoyed one incredible mishap after another. Outside of Newport, Arkansas, a wheel ran off the axle; we barely made our concert on time. There were numerous flats, each ruining the tire; we were never late for an engagement. Wheels broke, our axle bent, brakes and hitch gave much trouble because of the pianos' great weight. Finally, between Homer, Louisiana, and Mc-Comb, Mississippi, the trailer hitch parted, and I had the horrible thrill of seeing our trailer and pianos head over into a ditch.

It was a dreadful experience, but hardly an instant had passed before we went into action trying to salvage that evening's concert. On a dead run from the truck back toward the upturned trailer, I made plans. Down in the ditch, assessing our damage, I could hear Allison's low voice up above, saying, "Oh God, Oh God," over and over. Back in the truck, speeding toward the nearest town, we tried to keep little John from sensing that anything was wrong; indeed, this simulated cheerfulness helped to steady us, too.

Upon reaching town we split up in order to accomplish most in the least time (our evening's recital was still 150 miles away). Allison rode herd on a wrecker which went out to extricate the trailer, while I got some emergency welding done, and phoned ahead to warn a Baldwin dealer in Jackson, Mississippi, that we might need two pianos in a hurry that night if unloading disclosed ours to be unusable.

At McComb, Mississippi, we stuck to our policy of never ruining our sponsor's day by exposing him to our troubles; he had contracted for a concert, not a nervous breakdown. On the way to town, I hosed the fresh mud off the trailer; one fender, completely torn off, we hid under a rug in the truck; we made some excuse to our local contacts—perhaps that the accident had happened several days before. But would the pianos work? I phoned ahead for a piano technician to meet us in McComb, without telling our sponsors why.

The strain of wondering if our finely adjusted pianos were even half as torn up as the trailer was almost unbearable. Baldwin had told us these instruments were built to stand a beating. Did they mean a *beating*, or just a beating? For Allison the suspense was even worse. The moment we got to town, her assignment was to divert the welcoming committee so they would not be around and possibly disturbed when the pianos were uncovered.

After an hour of showing her the local azalea festival, they brought her back, white-faced but still smiling with ersatz cheer. I walked over and said quickly, "Everything is fine, and the pianos are in good shape," hoping it would seem only an idle pleasantry to the others. My poor wife almost wept with relief.

While I was sitting in bed ruminating thus cheerfully on the past, Allison dragged herself into a sitting position. She also tried to hang on to that last vestige of sleep by keeping one eye closed. One-eyed, we surveyed each other:

"Shall we hit it?" I queried.

"Wait. This is my time to sit."

"Wotzamatter?"

"I'm mad at you. Why did you have to wake me up?"

"We got to go."

"Mmmm."

Silence.

"Allison."

"Mmmm."

"What are you thinking about?"

"I'm ignoring you—that's what I'm thinking about."

Silence.

I looked down. My pants were on inside out. Why should that annoy me so?

I remembered the reception, only four hours ago. I remembered that the people at the reception were probably all still asleep. That annoyed me. I remembered what a good time I had had at the reception. That annoyed me. I had no business having a good time. Deliberately, I set about to think of something bad about that reception. Maybe I could hate somebody. Maybe that would make me feel better.

Before I knew it, John was up. With what you might call a vengeance. He was so bloody cheerful. He had gone to sleep at 7:10 the night before. I thought about that long night's sleep and almost hated him for it. In a few moments he was wolfing down a cold breakfast fetched out of the icebox which, along with a sink and stove, we had built into the truck. Lord, how he ate. But I was lucky, at that. If a child ate as much, comparatively, as a growing bird, he would consume three lambs and a calf in a single day. No wonder parent birds look so tired.

"Love, Daddy," gurgled John. I sent out a mental snarl, but some strange voice just below my eyes could be heard telling John how happy it made me to love him. Hmph. What a country. We don't even have freedom of speech any more.

While John ate, I folded our blankets and closed the bed back into a couch again. Preparing to shave, I opened a head-high cabinet door. We were parked on a slight slant; my razor and two plastic glasses fell off the shelf. "Damn." I bent down to pick up the dropped articles and cracked my head on the open door while rising. "*Damn.*"

"The next time somebody tells me how 'beautifully compact' this truck is," I snapped, "I'll strangle 'em. This thing is too damned cramped!"

I was right. From October to May, our family of three was living in an area (6' by 12') only two feet wider and three feet longer than our dining room table at home in Tennessee. Vengefully, I slammed the cabinet door. The one beside it flew open and a whole stack of pans went cascading to the floor. It was too much; one could not beat the truck; we were flexible and it was not. Dolefully, I stacked the pans back in their places and closed the door quietly.

After lathering my face, I leaned over the little sink to shave. A searing pain streaked across my jaw, snapping me wide awake. As cheap as razor blades are, why must I always try to make them last for a week? They nearly skin me alive on the fourth day. Grumbling, but awake by now, I changed blades.

Minutes later, our two-piece rig was cruising down the highway at fifty miles an hour. A motorist, spying the "Wave As You Pass!" sign on our trailer, honked gaily in passing. It almost made me feel good again.

If, by nursing several cups of coffee, we can just make it to nine o'clock in the morning, I'll usually run along quite well till about two o'clock the *next* morning—but late in the concert season, it's slow work getting up a head of steam.

It's a good thing we always leave town so quickly, I thought. If we stayed any longer, they'd find out what dull people we really are.

A few days later, we were home for the summer—and an exciting one it was to be. First, another two-piano team, who were good friends of ours, had surprised everyone by splitting up both maritally and musically. Their manager, André Mertens, asked if we would come to New York during the summer for an audition and to discuss a possible managerial contract.

Second, a free-lance writer had become interested in us and had sold the *Ladies' Home Journal* magazine an extensive feature on Allison and me. Mrs. Peta Fuller had heard us in Pinehurst, North Carolina, and was fascinated by the rolling home, piano moving and diaper changing. After interviewing us there in Pinehurst she asked for an "exclusive" on the story while she circulated the idea among a few magazines. The *Ladies' Home Journal* decided on us for its *How Young America Lives* series.

But it was the audition for Mr. Mertens which occupied most of our time and thought during the early summer.

Allison and I felt it likely that we were ready for a big New York management. For seven years, ever since I was twenty years old, we had been seasoning on television, in Australia, and for American regional managements. This was the year (1955) when Basil Rathbone observed that we had been wise in pacing our career; in Paris, Tennessee, for an appearance on the local artist series, he told us of Sir Henry Irving, who played fourteen years in small provincial theaters before even putting foot on a London stage. Our years of seasoning before audiences for whom mistakes might not necessarily be fatal were to stand us in good stead.

Planning for the audition, we tracked down gossip about Mr. Mertens. He was, it appeared, one of the few real impresarios in the country. Unlike most concert managers, who are sales people on only a speaking acquaintance with music, he was a perceptive man who really knew what he was listening to; as a result, he had a distinguished artist list. William Warfield and Jorge Bolet, close friends of ours, were under his management and spoke glowingly of him to us.

How does an expert, like Mertens, know "class" when he sees it?

Often it is in little clues the layman would think inconsequential. A building contractor once told me he enjoyed amazing his men by walking in on a job and picking out the good workmen almost instantly, hardly stopping to examine their work. How did he do it? "I always speak well of a carpenter," he said, "if, for instance, the slots on all his screw heads are turned in the same direction— in line with one another. Only a good craftsman will take pride in such small details." What pet details would a big manager look for? I didn't know, so we tried to anticipate everything.

In Homer, Louisiana (just before our trailer wreck), some high-school students had watched me unloading pianos. "Isn't he white?" tittered one of them. Not wanting to display a traditional "pianists' pallor," Allison and I spent weeks before our audition using sunlamps to simulate a healthy "golf-course glow." Perhaps Mr. Mertens would be sensitive about matters of dress. Wishing to make no mistakes, I sought professional advice. Out on tour, we went to a large clothing store. I asked for the head salesman.

"I want a suit," I told him, "which will look as though I can afford to buy any suit I want, but it must look as though I have too much taste to be flashy. I'll be wearing it on a moderately formal occasion where it will be seen by some hardboiled New York Yankees who know good clothes and style when they see them."

Without a moment's hesitation, he marched to a rack and pulled out the perfect suit. From that starting point we went over every article of dress which might be picked up by an observing eye. We bought a fine shirt, gray tie and socks (for that "prosperously restrained" look), a new watch band with matching cuff links and tie clip, a stylishly slim umbrella—and had my Homburg cleaned. Even articles to be carried in pockets, such as wallet and fountain pen, were bought new—in case they were ever taken out for any reason (signing contracts, for instance!). Allison's outfit was ordered by mail from an ad in *The New York Times,* to guarantee the currency of its style.

Carefully we calculated how many days before the audition I should get my hair cut so that it would look neat, but not self-consciously so—on how long my shoes should be worn to keep them from looking as though they were gotten just for the occasion. Would Mertens look at an artist's hands? I began to care for the condition of my nails.

Asked to play a half-hour audition, we wrote down and rehearsed our introductory comments and timed them, with the music, to exactly twenty-eight minutes; it is always better to be just a shade light on time. Mertens was Viennese and a good judge of musicianship; we opened with the exquisite *Fantasy in F minor* by Vienna's Franz Schubert. It was followed by a composition of Victor Babin's which we particularly enjoyed (his *Étude No. 1* for two pianos); Mr. Babin and his wife are the two-piano team of Vronsky and Babin, probably the best such ensemble playing today. If we could satisfy Mertens on our musicianship, we expected his next question to be, "Can these artists also appeal to laymen?" We scheduled some of our most popular encore material (a couple of the nonsensical *Variations on Yankee Doodle,* by Mario Braggiotti).

My former speech teacher, Mrs. Ruby Krider, listened to us rehearse the audition. She checked our speaking from the stage, our carriage when walking, how we were to sit in Mertens' office, and all those other details on which professionals sometimes imagine themselves beyond the need of coaching.

In strategy conferences with Dad, we chose our business positions with care. We decided not to tell Mertens that Allison was pregnant again, or that the *Ladies' Home Journal* was planning a feature on us. This last was surrendering a real bargaining point, but we felt it wise to do so: the *Journal* preferred not to advertise its plans; Mr. Mertens might think we were just talking big; and the possible

embarrassment if our story fell through for any reason, all justified
playing it close. Perhaps most of all, we wanted any new managers
to consider us solely on our natural assets.

Looking back, I believe we were overprepared, just as we had
been at Town Hall. Nothing, however, could bring me to advocate
less than a maximum effort on any professional matter. What
unlooked-for developments, or fear, may do to one's performance
he can never foresee; the only solution is to give each professional
effort everything you have. Only then will there be no regrets over
sins of omission.

The audition was so well rehearsed as to be anticlimactic. We
anticipated the thinking of our listeners so accurately that just as
I arose to announce our "light" pieces, they began asking if we
would "play something light." This little break I tried to exploit by
proceeding as though our next selections, and the few remarks I
had prepared, were spontaneous. (Which reminds me of the violinist
heard practicing an encore backstage. "What am I doing? I'm
practicing my spontaneity," he said.)

At our conference the following day, things went less well. Allison and I were grossing around $40,000 a year (though much of it
was used in keeping up with expenses) and felt reluctant to change
managements without some guarantees about money. Mertens felt
he could not make any. I asked if we might reserve a territory
for Ralph Bridges, to assure ourselves a meal ticket. Still no. Worst
of all, he felt strongly that we should stop carrying our son John
with us. It was "amateurish." He could not permit it; we, on the
other hand, were determined to keep our family life intact. Mertens was right from one point of view, but we felt we were just
as right. It was too bad.

Very often we work hard toward a goal, only to discover that
our ultimate rewards come, almost casually, from an entirely different source. One's work would almost seem to have been wasted,
were it not for the realization that no rewards would have come
without it. Before the collar on my good shirt had a chance to
get dirty, we went over to see Harlowe Dean at the Civic Concert
Service. You may remember that he had been encouraging us for
several years.

"How did the audition go?" he asked. I told him.

He set about to make us indebted to him forever. We had once told him he could have a chance at us when we were ready for a major New York management. Did that, he wondered, still go? Upon getting an affirmative answer, he took us down the hall to meet Phil Tippin, head of the Special Attractions Bureau of the National Artists Corporation. We did not know it yet, but we were just about to become a Special Attraction, whatever that was.

All details were quickly straightened out. We could carry sixteen children by wheelbarrow, so far as Phil Tippin cared, just as long as it didn't interfere with our work. He could make no guarantees about money, but out of respect for the loyalty which Ralph Bridges and I had shown each other, he would permit Alkahest to book us in the Southeast.

I had heard that big New York managers sometimes dictated programs to their artists. "How about that?" I asked.

"You're the artist," he replied, "not I. You handle all artistic matters. If I get complaints, you'll hear about it."

Phil has an interesting faculty for covering a lot of territory in a few words or phrases. He is one of those men who can write a short business letter, or can actually get all his business stated in a three minute long-distance call. I just don't understand people like that. All my letters are two pages long, and I have to talk about the weather for fifteen minutes before asking a simple question.

In that first conference, he said one thing which still lingers fragrantly in memory. I started to tell him a little about our background, and he said generously, "Oh, that's all right. I know about you through your reputation."

I protested that we did not yet have anything you could call a reputation.

"Oh, yes. I've run across you a lot. Nobody can play as much as you've played, and not have a reputation. It's quite good."

I liked it. If he could just make prospective sponsors vibrate about me the way I did about him just then, this was going to be all right.

At home in Paris, Tennessee, we settled down to await the arrival of our second child, expected in December. Unfortunately, God and the concert managers work on different schedules. Concerts are arranged as much as eighteen months in advance; babies turn up on shorter notice. Once again, our managers tore their hair over our cancellation of a fall tour. The resulting vacation was in name only, however. Much of the summer was devoted to helping the *Ladies' Home Journal* prepare their story on us.

At the end of the summer I went as an observer to a Civil Defense Staff College being held in Knoxville. The experience was frightening as well as enlightening. Paris had no Civil Defense organization, and after getting back I made many colorful speeches ("If you stood seven miles from an atomic explosion, the heat would *boil* the liquid in your eyeballs!") urging that the community do something. They appointed me Civil Defense Director for Henry County, and I have made no more speeches since then. This shows what a good thing Civil Defense can be for the country.

Allison and I always work hard with the local concert association when we are in town during its drives. We felt our time was overcrowded that fall, but who does not? And who will support music if musical people do not? Anyway, this self-crucifixion is a good way for us to understand what our sponsors go through to get us to all those towns where we play.

Sometimes I had been a little annoyed at the local contacts who met us warily, saying meaningfully, "You'd better be good . . ." After three weeks of hard, unpaid work on our concert association, I knew how it felt. When Basil Rathbone and Helen Gahagan Douglas got to Paris for the first program that year, I looked up across our dinner table and grinned, "You'd better be good . . ."

They thought I was joking.

At this time (October) I settled down to work in deadly earnest. All summer I had been trying to get time to write some two-piano transcriptions. This was the first time I could get enough privacy to concentrate. Without further ado, I gave myself up to an orgy of study and writing.

At such times Allison gives up on me. I worked all day and most of the night. I never shaved or washed; I smelled like a billy goat; my eyes became bloodshot and scratchy with strain; I ate little and seldom thanked her for that. I was kicked out of the upstairs bedroom and slept in my office without changing clothes for two weeks running.

Coming up for air, I presented Allison with some valuable additions to our repertoire. I had started the project because two works we wished to play were not adequately transcribed for two pianos (the *Mephisto Waltz* of Liszt, and Bach's *Toccata and Fugue in D minor*); at least, I did not feel the existing transcriptions were sufficiently faithful to the composers' original intentions. My work had been slow, but the final products proved to be two of the most successful offerings we have ever used on tour.

On December 12, 1955, Mary Catharine Neal was born. She was lovingly named for Mrs. Mary Zimbalist (who founded the Curtis Institute) and Mrs. Catharine Wright (in whose home we were married). Three weeks later, the little infant flew with us to New York, where we did a week's promotional work just as our story was released in the *Ladies' Home Journal*. In this family they start early.

We had asked Ralph Bridges to cancel all our fall bookings that season, so Allison could rest while waiting for her second child. It was a wise decision, but we had not rested.

Perhaps we were drunk with power. Perhaps we believed our strength was unlimited. We had so long scorned the people who are always saying that you "can't" do this or that, that we began to think there was nothing we could not force our bodies to do—that we could, with impunity, push our bodies to any lengths. Refusal to coddle oneself may be a great strength. Failure to take care of oneself can be a tragic mistake.

For us, this bitter lesson lay just ahead.

Allison and I played intensively that spring.

Overconfident of our strength, we ignored the additional strain which had been placed on our vitality by carrying two children instead of one. We never permitted personal indisposition to interfere with our programs, so what was there to worry about?

By early February, we were tired. My legs had that heavy feeling usually reserved for the month of April. This should have been a warning signal; we were already exhausted after only a few weeks on the road. In Florida Allison developed a cold; she ignored it. Instead of using days off for resting, she washed our dirty clothes at Ralph Bridges' house in Atlanta; this questionable economy saved us perhaps $6.00 while chilling and tiring Allison badly. By Gainesville, Georgia, the cold was intestinal flu; by Dalton, Georgia, it was bronchitis; by Shelbyville, Tennessee, she had developed a strong reaction to some antibiotics taken for a kidney

infection. After our recital in Shelbyville she trembled and wept
without apparent reason.

Still, we thought we could keep going. I called Mother, who took
a taxi all the way across the state (I shudder to remember the
bill!) to take our children home. It was all in vain, for in Chat-
tanooga the next night, Allison collapsed backstage while a large
audience sat out front waiting. Sometimes, we learned bitterly, the
show does not go on. We canceled the next leg of our tour and
went home to rest and think things over.

The doctors' verdict was unanimous: Exhaustion. Was André
Mertens right? Was everyone else right? Must we give up either
our career or our ideals about family life? More than anything, I
wanted my wife to be happy. How could she and I have our cake
and eat it, too? We loved both our career and our children. Must
we choose between them?

It did not take me long to decide that our only hope for a
solution lay in a long-time dream, which I had thus far ignored
because of the very great expense involved. This dream was to
have a huge, custom-built bus, outfitted with completely self-
sufficient living quarters, and which would also carry a chauffeur
and maid to relieve us of driving, piano loading and housekeeping.

Such a vehicle would also relieve me of one nagging concern
which had worried me ever since we first thought of carrying
children on the road. In the fall of 1951, Allison and I had been
snowbound in a Missouri blizzard. All day we sat in a line of
some four hundred cars, unable to move in either direction. Periodically, a state patrolman walked up and down the line, asking
people to turn off the car motors they had started, trying to get a
little heat. Suddenly word sped down the line that somewhere up
ahead a baby had become violently ill; it had a high fever, no
food, and unsatisfactory heat. There was fear for its life. For years
I had wondered what happened to that baby, out on the road, away
from heat and food. This new bus would at least assure us of
having all the facilities of home with us wherever we were.

Sometimes I used to wonder about entertainment personalities
who earned considerable sums of money, but always ended up
broke. My dream bus, hereinafter known as Neal's Folly, was to
teach me how very easily this can happen.

I wrote to a leading custom bus manufacturer and asked for a bus of a size small enough to go anywhere in the country without special permits, but still large enough to carry the following equipment: two concert grand pianos, thermostatic heat, air conditioning, a complete bathroom—including tub (babies cannot use a shower), a complete kitchen—including a three-burner stove with oven, double sink and electric refrigerator, a 5,000-watt electric generator which would start automatically whenever an appliance was turned on, sleeping quarters for eight (married people sometimes keep on having children!) and their wardrobes. I wished everything to be self-contained in regard to fuel and water supplies, sewage disposal tanks, etc. On the highway, Neal's Folly must have all the facilities of home. Except space.

They wrote back and told me that what I asked for was impossible. That much equipment could not possibly be gotten into a 35-foot bus. As is common with those who cry "can't," they had many fine reasons to support their point of view. All the builders I wrote and visited made similar statements, submitting bids on alternate equipment all the way up to $52,000.

As with papering our house, we finally got mad and designed the bus ourselves. It was an education in engineering. When we got through, the bus contained everything we had asked for, was amazingly compact (Allison now loves to inspect house trailers, exclaiming about their "waste space"), and had taken nearly a whole summer's planning. Sometime, just for fun, try to design a bathroom containing a toilet, tub, basin, two cupboards, and a full length closet—all within an area of 40″ by 58″ and over a wheel-housing to boot!

As if the summer weren't already enough of a financial mess, my dear wife chose this moment to tell me she needed a new coat. We were preparing to go on our first tour for the National Artists Corporation, and she wanted a nice, new coat. She was quite reasonable, really, mentioning prices of about $75 or $80.

That was when I made my mistake. I started to get fancy. In a New York paper I saw an ad for a wonderful coat of synthetic fabric. The ad ran something like this: "It looks like mink; it feels like mink; you'll think it is mink." The price was $135, a little more than I had intended spending—but then, nothing's too good for the little woman. Besides, how wonderful it would be to fool our clients into thinking Allison had a real mink coat. I sent in an

order saying it had better look like mink. It came. Allison met me
with a dolorous expression.

"What's the matter, dear?" I asked.

Whenever Allison is faced with a sad, unanswerable situation,
she always moans, "As Roy Dumas (our colored yard man) says
so beautifully, 'Well'um.' "

It didn't look like mink. It didn't feel like mink. Nobody was
ever going to think it was mink. One will ask, "Why worry? Why
not just return this mistake and buy the coat you originally intended?" I'll tell you why. Because of female chemistry. I had
started the mink foolishness, and now my bride meant to have
mink and no maybes about it. If I could have that bus (notice, the
bus is "mine" now) she could have a mink. So.

After much shopping, I ordered a lovely stole which just matched
the color of Allison's hair. It's just a business investment, I told
myself, but I was more excited about that fur than Allison. Waiting for it to come, I secretly met every train coming into town,
whether it came at midday, in the middle of the night, or just
before dawn. The house was asleep the morning I got home with
that slim little package. Soon lights were flicking on, and little
yelps of joy could be heard from one room after another as Allison
pranced about in her pajamas, modeling the stole and showing off
for the family.

"Of course," she said preening, trying to make peace with her
frugal instincts, "it's just a business investment, isn't it?"

Well, maybe.

This (1956-57) was a concert season we had spent years waiting
for.

Our schedule included ninety-six engagements, which was about
par for us, but for the first time we were playing for a major
management. Often, the qualities which make one successful in
the minor leagues show up very poorly when one gets to the Big
Time. This also works in reverse: the qualities which make a
big-time radio man or medical specialist successful may do him
little good in a small town radio station or medical practice. Allison and I had made every possible effort to equip ourselves for
a move into the big league. We wanted to justify Harlowe Dean's
faith in us.

We were thoroughly prepared musically. We were hocked to our eyeballs to buy a vast bus which was designed to give us every comfort of home while on the road. A chauffeur and maid were to relieve us of all considerations but those of playing the piano. We had laid what I believe to have been the best of plans.

The best of plans go awry.

First, I repeated my old mistake of trying to economize when hiring help. I hired Tom and Rosie. Looking back, I must admit they showed up well in my interviews and investigations. Rosie was a domestic who had worked in good homes for twenty years. Tom was a truck driver and had many years' experience making the run from Chicago to the South. Both had a reputation for honesty, no drinking, no gambling, no nothing. They seemed the perfect answer.

On the debit side, Rosie was so fat it took fifteen minutes to walk around her. When she marched down the narrow aisle of our bus, she swept everyone and everything before her. Our bathtub was twenty-two inches wide; I will guess Rosie was thirty-two inches wide. At first we contemplated rigging a block and tackle from the ceiling, and then I wasted some moments wondering whether she did one half of her body at a time. I needn't have worried. Rosie untied the Gordian knot with an Alexandrian stroke: she never bathed on our journeys.

His wife might not bathe in day-to-day living, but Tom was marvelously fastidious whenever an emergency arose. A fire broke out underneath the bus, and Tom hovered about dangling the fire extinguisher uselessly in one hand, because it would dirty his uniform to crawl under the rig. Allison and I did all the crawling that was done under *that* bus.

As a driver, Tom did not improve with age. True, local people often complimented him, but in that regard I observe that ineptitude looks hard. I have often been complimented after taking four clumsy cuts to park the bus, while no one ever notices if I place it in one smooth motion—that looks too easy. Tom's eyes never moved in their sockets; his whole head rotated from the neck, even when just looking across the page of a book. He drove that way, too, hunched over the steering wheel, eyes straight ahead, never looking to the right nor to the left. When Tom came to a curve, his eyes never anticipated, or turned with the road, but kept straight in line with the bus, like headlights. At such times he never turned the steering wheel freely, with a hand-over-hand motion, but made innumerable jerky little half turns, as a nervous woman does with her husband's car. Watching him drive was far worse than doing it ourselves.

Tom was advertised as being "mechanical." He could "fix things." One day he came to me, asking for a screwdriver.

"Why?" I asked.

"The motor's stripped a gear, and I have to fix it," he said.

Perhaps we should have been grateful for the presence of such a mechanical genius. Our bus, incidentally, had a Hydramatic Transmission; Tom explained to strangers that he was driving a shiftless bus.

No catastrophe could arise but what we learned that Tom had "been afraid of that," and no instructions could be given for future action without his replying, "I been thinkin' 'bout that." If I asked Tom how far we had driven that day, his reply was invariably, "Not sure, exactly, but a right smart little ways." Let me ask the name of any town we had just passed through, and I was informed, "Don't rightly know, but it's a right smart-sized town."

The terrible truth dawned on me. Tom knew the route to Chicago by sight, but in spite of his claims he could not operate with maps on strange roads. The final straw came when our bus and we were all aboard an ocean-going ferry on our way to Martha's Vineyard, seven miles off the coast of Massachusetts.

"Tom," I demanded, "where are we?"

"Well, I don't rightly know, suh. Don't know as I heard you say."

"Do you even know what that is?" I cried, pointing at the Atlantic Ocean.

"Sure," he answered, with injured pride. Then, hesitantly, "Lake Mitch-igan?"

Perhaps Tom and Rosie were the least of our troubles.

The Folly, in which had been sunk so much grocery money, was an unending agony throughout the fall. I had spared nothing to make it the last word in trouble-free transportation. Every conceivable thing went wrong. In the first place, the contractor entrusted with outfitting the bus did not finish his job on time. My truck and trailer had already been sold to another two-piano team, so we had to use the new bus, ready or not. It wasn't. At the last moment we had to chase out still-working carpenters, throw our belongings willy-nilly into the bus and take off with wood shavings, spare doors and uninstalled equipment lying all over the floor.

About 360 miles away, we caught on fire. By amazing good fortune, we were almost directly in front of a fire station in downtown Cincinnati when it happened. The trouble was caused by improper wiring, which would take two days to correct. We had a concert scheduled for that night in Alma, Michigan.

Allison's fingers had been burned badly in the fire (she tried to pull a smoldering cable loose with her bare hands), but the finger tips themselves were not blistered; I telephoned our sponsor in Alma, advising him that local pianos must be obtained for the recital that night, and we grabbed a plane for Michigan. Somewhere—I think it was Toledo—we arrived so late that our connecting plane had closed its doors and was pulling out to the runway. I have never seen Allison more determined. Helplessly watching the plane start to move, I was amazed to see my trim little spouse running out across the asphalt, waving her arms at the pilot. Grinning, he stopped the plane; a portable stairway was rolled out, the doors opened, and we were back in business again.

Our recital went well that night. Off stage, Allison kept her hands covered to hide them from our sponsor's eyes. For once, however, we were not successful in keeping our troubles a complete secret. After the concert, we were taken out to supper. Allison's blisters were so placed that she could not use pressure on a knife and fork, and had to ask me to cut her food. I think she enjoyed the look on our hosts' faces when they saw her hands.

From a bad beginning, things got worse.

Our water tanks leaked. The electrical system gave trouble. Our toilet overflowed and soaked the blankets which were lying all over the floor (the cabinets in which they should have been placed were unfinished). The propane gas system froze up every day or two, so that we had no heat, no stove, no hot water, no nothing. Huddled in overcoats, we watched the snow outside and shivered. Bitterly, I remembered all our talk the previous summer, looking forward to our "wonderful, trouble-free mobile unit." The old truck and trailer had been better than this!

When I called up our sponsors from a hundred miles down the

road, I must have left them wondering what was coming to town. First I settled the piano-moving time; then I asked if they could get me a carpenter or cabinet shop on short notice; next I asked for a plumber, an electrician, or a propane gas company. Even the bus itself gave us trouble. The right front brake locked almost every day, seeming to defy adequate repair. A cylinder head cracked. The generator burned out. The automatic transmission had to be torn out and rebuilt. A week later the job had to be repeated. Shortly afterwards, the motor had to be overhauled.

Looking back through all those incredible bills and receipts, I am amazed that we stayed on the road. Through it all, we were never late for an engagement, and we never permitted our personal problems to disturb our clients or to follow us on stage.

Don't feel too sorry for us. Other artists have problems, too.

They are made uncomfortable by poor hotel accommodations; we sleep in the same comfortable bed every night. They are half-poisoned by roadside cooking; we carry our own kitchen. Their stomachs are upset by strange water; we carry our own water from city to city. They struggle with suitcases and packing every day; we do not. Strange train and plane connections disrupt their living hours. We may travel, heart in mouth, wondering if our transmission will blow up, but they ride, heart in mouth, wondering if the train engineer, running late, will make up enough time to meet their next connection.

One problem we never have any more is the 2:55 a.m. train after a recital, which usually means no sleep for the artist. Even worse is the notorious 10:38 p.m. train; at four or five towns every year we hear of some artist having insulted the audience by racing through his program, omitting repeats or movements, substituting shorter pieces, and skipping encores, all in order to make that early train.

Of course it was the big problem of family life which motivated us in building the bus. Try to imagine the frustrated instincts of the concert artist who does not see his children for half a year at a time—and imagine what nervous hellions his children are. I, on the other hand, see far more of my children than the average man does who works in an office all day. Not one day goes by but what my children are well loved, well spanked and well enjoyed.

Allison and I have problems, to be sure, but we have deliberately

chosen those problems in preference to others. Feel sorry for somebody else.

However, when we limped home in Christmas of 1956, we did
not feel philosophical. We seemed to have been failures. All our
plans had gone awry. Neal's Folly, instead of solving problems, had
created monumental new ones. Our help, instead of relieving us
of work and responsibility, had simply added to the demands of
travel. I was distressed and unhappy. Was this comic-opera farce
really justifying Harlowe Dean's faith in us? Were we just fooling
ourselves in believing that our work was not suffering because of
our personal lives?

We used the holidays to patch up the bus and look for new
help. No one could be located on such short notice, and we had
to go back on the road alone, hopelessly asking about drivers in
each town we visited.

It was a blue Christmas.

After Christmas, life seemed to settle down a bit. We had some
luck in hiring temporary drivers from bus companies in different
parts of the country. We had little time to investigate these people,
however, and we discovered sadly that when a man was willing
to leave town on short notice, it usually meant there was something
wrong with him. But I had some sympathies for the men, too.
Heaven knows how our touring appeared to them. They seldom
understood what we were doing, called every work we played a
"song," and wouldn't have been caught dead listening to one of our
recitals.

On tour, as in all life, it is the little things which erode one's
patience down into exasperation. Eating, for instance, is a simple
operation which must happen three times each day. Imagine the
case of Donald Bryant, director of the famed Columbus Boychoir.

"Your little boy may knock over a glass of milk once a week," he
told me, "making once every twenty-one meals. We have a whole
bus-load of children on the road together, which means that at
least one glass of milk is knocked over at every meal! Toward the
end of the tour I begin to get desperate, and think they're doing
it deliberately, and swear I'll kill the next one that does it!"

What I usually notice about eating on the road is that we never
get to the good places. We've played four recitals in New Orleans;

our friends invariably ask about the wonderful restaurants for which that city is famous, but we have never had time for those places. Whenever we go out to eat, we just walk hurriedly into a roadside eatery and ask, "What's ready?" It's always roast beef. How I hate roast beef.

Allison says that her picture is a little different. "There's the story of my life:" she says, "trying to get my lipstick on straight while bumping down the highway." She spends her spare highway time working crossword puzzles ("I always have to cheat, and look in the back of the book, to make them come out").

But Allison and I are musicians. In the final analysis, none of our touring problems is pertinent, except those which have bearing on the piano.

One of the artistic controversies of touring in America is the current practice of using a single program throughout an entire season. This is certainly not an ideal situation, though it is not quite so unique and diabolical as some artists insist they believe. Actors have an identical situation when taking part in a play which enjoys an extended run. Nobody weeps for the actors, and I don't weep for the musicians. Indeed, a good work of art can stand an almost indefinite amount of study and contemplation; personally, I enjoy living intimately with my repertoire.

While doing an extended run in *Middle of the Night*, Edward G. Robinson was asked, "How does it feel to do the same thing every night?" His reply stated the problem exactly: "The difficult thing is to do it for the first time every night."

Once before, I mentioned the tendency, in performance, to change one's rehearsed pattern by making small exaggerations of effects. These exaggerations, if uncontrolled, could soon distort his performances. I asked Basil Rathbone about this problem of performance and rehearsal.

"I understand perfectly," he replied. "The best director I ever worked under used to call the cast together periodically for a rehearsal, beginning with the words, 'All right, let's take out all the improvements!'" The attainment of simplicity, as Vengerova said, is very often the most difficult thing of all.

Audiences imagine physical considerations to be difficult. Allison smashed a thumb five minutes before playing in Benton, Arkansas, and had to refinger all the *glissandos* in Ravel's *La Valse* on the spot. Once I ripped a thumbnail viciously while performing the Rachmaninoff *Tears*. During a brief solo by Allison I had to tear the nail off through the skin to get it so I could play. When I arose, my keyboard was smeared with blood. It hurt like hell, but these are not the real problems of playing on tour, however much a layman might be impressed.

One of my problems used to be that I started to play without stopping to think about the music first. As a result, my openings were often weak and erratic. Finally, regardless of how it looked to the audience, I began to pause before each important work for a moment of self-dedication and projection into the music. To my surprise, it prepared not only me, but the audience as well.

"What are you doing when you bow your head?" I am often asked. "Praying?"

It is entirely possible that we are, though not in a conventional sense. I do know that it is a moment when the world falls away and when Allison and I are left alone with each other and with the music.

And that is what we live for.

Once again spring arrived, flowers blossomed in Tennessee, and I carried my little family back home.

We were eager to know how our New York managers felt about the tour. We believed our work to have been very good, but people are notoriously poor judges of themselves. I still had a sour taste in my mouth over the poor start we had made in the fall, and constantly wondered what sort of reports had gone back to New York. Presently Phil Tippin sent me a large sheaf of newspaper reviews, which the National Artists Corporation had collected during our first tour for them. Allison and I travel so fast that we almost never stay in a town long enough to see these reports, and we went over them avidly.

One of the quickest ways for an artist to go downhill is to believe his newspaper notices. Still, they are a good indication of one's general reception, and as such we were gratified to see that our press criticism had, without exception, been more than kind. We were particularly relieved to see that none of the reviews reflected our personal difficulties during the fall tour. Commenting about a freak accident on stage (I had to stop the concert and crawl under my piano to fix a broken pedal), the *Schenectady* (New York) *Gazette* unwittingly summed up our entire fall tour with the observation that "Nelson and Neal are true troupers and fortunately nothing upsets them too much."

At Martha's Vineyard, where Tom exasperated me by thinking we were crossing "Lake Mitch-igan," the *Vineyard Gazette* began its account of our recital with the opinion that "It seems unlikely that any concert ever presented on the Vineyard has been the subject of more adulatory comment than that presented by Nelson and Neal."

In Newport, Rhode Island, where we were upset by mechanical failures in the bus, *The News* spoke of our "spectacular playing," which "evoked spontaneous and prolonged applause." In Latrobe, Pennsylvania, our refrigerator wouldn't run, the electric generator stopped going, and our gas system froze up—leaving us so cold and angry with frustration that I called up my parents in Tennessee just to have someone to cuss at. We didn't take it out on our clients, though; the local *Bulletin* said our "audience was entranced."

Tom, my Phi Beta Kappa driver, got lost four times in twenty miles, almost driving us to distraction with fear of being late, but once on stage, the Akron *Beacon-Journal* said we "captivated the audience." Even in Portsmouth, Ohio, where I was violently ill from some kind of food poisoning, the *Portsmouth Times* ran a headline, "Audience Thrilled by Duo," commenting that we had earned a "notable success, meriting every round of applause from a thrilled audience that demanded five encores."

Our troubles had calmed down after Christmas, but we had already profited richly from those years of seasoning under smaller managements. Basil Rathbone, an old pro, had assured us that we would one day be grateful for that seasoning. He was right; when we began touring for a major management, we were not flustered by small annoyances, and had discipline and control enough so that personal considerations were never allowed to interfere with our professional work.

Perhaps the most apt comment of our whole tour was that of the Dayton (Ohio) *Daily News*, which said that " 'Bach, babies and

Beethoven' fit the Neals' living pattern." Neither they nor we knew it, but another baby was soon to be on the way. Allison Elise Neal joined our family in December of 1957.

She seems a happy child.

I have spent most of my life imagining that if I could just get over that one next hurdle, all our troubles would be over. Then happiness would set in.

At first it was getting a good education; then, any kind of a start in professional music; then, a manager; next, a big manager, or a bigger bus to live in on the road. None of these developments ended anything. Instead they introduced us to new problems and hurdles. Early in the game I got the idea that happiness was an absence of problems, and lay just beyond the next objective.

All my life had been spent in enduring, or putting up with today, while waiting for a fulfilled and happy tomorrow. But there are always goals, and he who seeks happiness in the form of immediate goals is doomed to frustration.

One night that summer, I lay in bed beside Allison, listening to our children whisper noisily in the next room, and suddenly realized that this was happiness right now; that happiness has always been in striving toward our goals, and not in their final achievement. We had just completed our first season on the national concert circuits. The press had been kind, our sponsors were pleased, and our managers raised our fees; but still we were in the midst of problems.

For instance, Allison and I had played 661 concerts on two continents in the past seven years. According to Frederick Schang, president of Columbia Artists Management, there are about 10,000 concert opportunities (more than in all the rest of the world put together) available to artists in North America each year. Many of these opportunities are rigidly controlled by various managements, thus severely limiting the number available to any one artist. The performing average, based on an estimate of some 300 competing artists (who may be called "successful"), is about thirty dates for each artist per year. For seven years, Allison and I had gobbled up about three times that average. Clearly, we might be in some danger of wearing out the available market, unless many of our former clients were kind enough to ask for us back again.

Still, we have learned to live with the idea that our career could disintegrate completely within any given year. If the public were to grow tired of us; if we were to fail in our responsibilities to them; or if any number of other professional developments arose, it could wipe us out altogether. This uncertainty, however, is not unique to us or to artists in general. Every professional man knows it, and even the corner grocer could be crowded out suddenly by a hard-working newcomer next door. Security lies within the individual himself, and not in his external circumstances. Allison and I work hard, have faith, and are at peace with the world.

We love each other, playing together, and we love the two-piano medium. In the late piano works of such composers as Beethoven and Brahms you can hear them struggling with the limitations of what only ten fingers can do on a keyboard. It is small wonder, then, that many composers in their mature years turned toward chamber music. This was a form expanded beyond the possibilities of a solo instrument, yet limited enough that the composer was never overstretched technically. Conceived as chamber music, two-piano playing is a gratifying art form.

But we still have problems. As I write this, Allison and I are out on the road in northern Pennsylvania, waiting for her to recover from an attack of the mumps. To make matters worse, she caught the mumps from me.

My attack was a dreadful thing which caught us in West Texas. Allison put me to bed and drove the bus 1,100 miles to Florida, hoping I would be able to play when we got there; however I became desperately ill and still more concerts had to be postponed or canceled. Between her mumps and mine, our tour was a heartbreaking mess. Few things can be as lonely as enduring troubles far from home. Even so, you couldn't get us to change our way of life for anything in the world.

We're just sitting here, champing at the bit, dying to start playing again. The moment that doctor says Allison is ready to go, we're going to grab the kids, jump in the bus, and hit the highway. Don't forget: If you see us on the road,

Wave As You Pass!

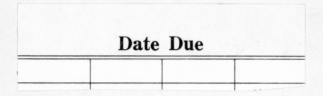